Carlos Sainz and Luis Moya take a small jump in the 2001 Safari Rally in their Ford Focus WRC. The Safari is traditionally a car (and driver) breaker, with far fewer than half of the starting order making it to the finish. (Mike Gibbon, MVG Photographic)

Fit
for
motor
sport

IMPROVE YOUR RACE PERFORMANCE WITH
BETTER PHYSICAL AND MENTAL TRAINING

With a chapter on motorsport medical emergency procedures

Dr R S **Jutley** BSc, MB, ChB, MRCS

Foreword by Professor **Sid Watkins** MD, FRCS
and contributions by
Bernie Shrosbree, Human Performance Manager, Renault Formula 1
Louise Aitken-Walker MBE, 1990 FIA World Ladies Rally Champion

To my parents, Harjinder Singh and Mohinder Kaur,
to whom I am irretrievably indebted

First published in January 2003

A catalogue record for this book is
available from the British Library

ISBN 1 85960 876 0

Library of Congress control no. 2002110159

Published by Haynes Publishing, Sparkford,
Yeovil, Somerset BA22 7JJ, UK
Tel: 01963 442030 Fax: 01963 440001
Int. tel: +44 1963 442030 Int. fax: +44 1963 440001
E-mail: sales@haynes-manuals.co.uk
Website: www.haynes.co.uk

Haynes North America Inc.,
861 Lawrence Drive, Newbury Park,
California 91320, USA

Page layout by G&M Designs Limited, Raunds, Northamptonshire
Printed and bound in Britain by J. H. Haynes & Co. Ltd, Sparkford

Contents

Foreword
by Professor Sid Watkins MD, FRCS

President of the Medical Commission FIA, President of the Research Commission FIA, President of the Safety Commission FIA, and Formula One Medical Delegate FIA

Dr Jutley has written a very useful book containing a great deal of information and excellent advice. The book, though primarily written to improve motorsport performance, is pertinent to many sports and activities and, indeed, to ordinary daily living.

In the section on weight loss I found myself checking my height and weight and reaching for a calculator to determine whether I was obese or morbidly obese. In fact, to my relief, my Body Mass Index (BMI) placed me merely into the overweight variety. But this inspired me to calculate my Resting Metabolic Rate (RMR), my daily energy expenditure and the necessary reduction in calorific intake to return to my svelte and youthful figure.

In the section on 'The event', extremely valuable guidance is given on diet and hydration. The maintenance of a sufficient fluid intake during performance in racing conditions with a high thermal load is of vital importance and is properly stressed.

Finally the book contains a section on emergency care in motorsport and on rescue. This should be mandatory knowledge for the man or woman in the street let alone motorsport competitors. The illustrations on page 121 tell a salutary and cautionary tale concerning the need to improve standards.

I enjoyed reading Dr Jutley's book very much. I am sure this pleasure will be shared with all of its readers, who will, in addition, acquire the knowledge to improve their own fitness and performance in life regardless of their vocations or occupations.

November 2002
Sabael
New York

A word from David Lloyd

A Mitsubishi Ralliart Evo VI negotiates a stage of the 2001 Safari Rally in Kenya. Not uncommonly, outside temperatures exceed 30°C, with cockpit temperatures as high as 55°C. This places great stresses on the competitors, many of whom succumb to heat stroke and dehydration. (Mike Gibbon, MVG Photographic)

The staff at Next Generation Clubs and I are delighted to be associated with Dr Raj Jutley's book *Fit for Motorsport*. I have been involved in sport and fitness nearly all my life and recognise the importance of both training and safety in the pursuit of sporting excellence. This book offers a unique insight into both these aspects of motorsport. Rally driving, by its very nature, can be dangerous and few understand the potential hazards more than the drivers and the emergency doctors. Dr Jutley has filled both these roles.

From experience such as the Safari Rally he is able to give the reader simple and concise doctrines for better mental and physical preparation, as well as advising how to cope with emergencies should these occur. His recommendations are backed by several top competitors and fitness personalities such as Colin McRae, Jim Moodie and Bernie Shrosbree. Next Generation's own health and fitness expert Malcolm McPhail was also involved in the book's compilation. I recommend *Fit for*

Motorsport as a valuable addition to the collection of any motorsport driver or enthusiast – past, present or future.

David Lloyd
Chairman, Next Generation Clubs
December 2002

Introduction

Physical and mental fitness are now buzz words in just about every human pursuit, and it's no surprise, perhaps, that North America was quickest to spot the link between personal performance and fitness, not only in sport but also in everyday work. Indeed, it's not uncommon to find fully-fitted gyms and clinical psychologists readily available to staff in large US corporations – and, sure enough, productivity has increased.

It has long been realised, of course, that peak fitness is a prerequisite for a competitive edge in sport, but it could be argued that over the years most of those in motorsport have tended to ignore it. Even in Formula 1 racing, not so long ago, there were instances of drivers being exhausted and severely dehydrated, and quite often they would need help to simply get out of the car at the end of a race. Possibly the most memorable incident was Nelson Piquet collapsing on the podium at the Brazilian Grand Prix in 1982. In fact, that incident was probably what led FISA, motorsport's governing body at the time, to look seriously into driver performance and fitness. In motorsport, fitness is not just about driving faster, it's about driving more safely – about making fewer mistakes, which, at worst, could prove disastrous for driver, other competitors and spectators.

Over recent years the fitness of their drivers has become increasingly important to the Formula 1 teams and top rally outfits and they now routinely employ team doctors, physiotherapists, physiologists,

David Coulthard returning to the pits after a run round the circuit. (Mike Gibbon, MVG Photographic)

psychologists, dieticians and even ex-armed forces personnel to increase levels of mental and physical fitness. The Renault Formula 1 team has a Human Performance Laboratory, housed in a separate building at their Oxford headquarters, that would shame some of the best-equipped gyms. There's no doubt that the top drivers now have fitness levels comparable to top-class athletes. Sadly, though, the opposite is generally true for amateur competitors (hugely larger in number) who – like most of those living in developed countries – have a tendency to be overweight and in need of regular exercise. The race and rally cars available to them, on the other hand, are becoming more powerful and faster, and the competition tighter and fiercer. This combination is highly likely to lead to problems, and there are indeed problems.

I find that even amongst those competing in club and national motorsport events there are many instances of drivers being ill-prepared both physically and mentally. It's not unusual to see a driver make a fantastic start to an event only to fade as the day progresses, and the reason is usually that they are unaware of, or have been badly advised on, how to prepare for the event – for instance, what particular components of fitness to concentrate on and how to develop the components most likely to be stressed during the event. This can lead to retirement from or even crashing out of events – which is rather an expensive way of competing!

In 1998 I drove in my first Safari Rally,

Peak fitness is a prerequisite for a competitive edge. (Sporting Pictures UK)

a round of the FIA World Rally Championship, and I felt that I was pretty fit, having climbed to the summit of a 20,000ft mountain only months before. I paid little attention to preparing myself for this arduous race over three days covering 2,500km in temperatures often around 30°C, and on the third stage, some 600km into the first day, I was time-barred for not finishing within the allocated period. The reason was simply that I was physically and mentally fatigued and suffering from dehydration from my failure to plan my fluid and food intake. I learnt from these mistakes, and since then my participation in subsequent Safari Rallies, although as tough as ever, has been a thoroughly enjoyable experience.

It is my own personal experience and my observation of the experiences of many other competitors that inspired me to write this book. In it I have tried to explain as clearly as possible the principles of training for fitness. Although the fitness industry remains one of the fastest expanding industries in the world there is a lot of confusion over terminology, training principles and the basic concepts of fitness, and the innumerable websites set up by self-professed experts on the Internet haven't helped. Many of their *magic*

formulae for instant weight loss are based on poor scientific principles that can actually harm the body rather than achieve what they claim.

So what does this book provide? It provides the reader with simple, established and safe training principles. It is not a substitute for skill, so it is not designed to make you into a Colin McRae, a Louise Aitken-Walker or a Jenson Button, but it will give you an insight into how they train and prepare for their races. My aim is not to show you how to drive but how to maximise your driving by preparing yourself better both mentally and physically. Each chapter deals with a particular aspect of fitness and gives motorsport-specific advice on how to assess and develop it. There is also a chapter on emergencies, a subject which I consider an important part of any motorsport competitor's knowledge. Fortunately emergencies are relatively uncommon but when they do occur they can be very dramatic, and I provide an insight into what motorsport emergency procedures involve, so that if they do happen drivers are informed and co-operative with the rescue team.

I hope you enjoy reading the book as much as I have enjoyed writing it.

Acknowledgements

As with most such publications there are many people who provided their time, skills and resources to bring what started as a scribbled idea to a published book. Special thanks go to Dave 'Sid' Simpson, Crew Chief of Granite Rescue for his ebullience; his company of Graham Bruce, Stu Castleton, Steve Wright, Anne-Marie Cassidy, Cpl Roger 'Dinger' Bell; the Shire Rescue crew of Brian Hatton and Steve; Roy Smith and Jamie Smith for loan of their rally car; Dr John Harrington, Chief Medical Officer, Speyside Rally, Snowman Rally and Colin McRae Forest Stages; Aman Agarwal of Harvey's, Edinburgh; Paul Lewis in Aberdeen for legal advice; Sarah Hughes for IT skills and Fiona Walsh. I am also grateful to David Lloyd, Patrick Coote, Malcolm McPhail and the staff of Next Generation Clubs and Life Fitness for supporting the fitness sections; Hayleigh Maxfield and Naveed Iqbal of www.worldrallying.com.

Special thanks go to those who contributed their professional material and skills: Mike Gibbon of MVG Photographic, also for his enthusiasm; Maurice Selden and Martin Holmes of Martin Holmes Rallying; Colin McMaster of McKlein; Anwar Sidi of Sidi's Photography, Kenya; Dr David Nelson of Quotronics Systems; Sarah Blackham and the PR staff of Renault F1; Sarah Christofi and Barbara Serhant of Red Bull; Servier Laboratories Limited; Human Kinetics; Crowood Press; Calorie Control Council and the RAF Lossiemouth Photographic Section who kindly supported the emergency section shots.

Special acknowledgements are due to the following for their individual contributions and help in pushing the right buttons. First, the McRaes who need no introduction: Jim McRae and Colin McRae MBE; Bernie Shrosbree, Human Performance Manager, Renault F1; Louise Aitken-Walker MBE, Jim Moodie, Iain McPherson, Robbie Head of Channel 4 WRC, Victor Morgan of VM Sports Agencies; Colin Wilson of the MSA; Dr John Harrington, Dr David Cranston, Dr Rob Johnston, Dr Matt Smith, Jan Gibbon, Lynne Howe-Green and Tina Biddlecombe.

I am particularly grateful to Ken Walker, chairman of the MSA medical advisory committee, who read and commented on the original manuscript, and to Prof Sid Watkins for his superb Foreword. My thanks also to the staff at Haynes Publishing, especially Mark Hughes for seeing the potential in the book, and Flora Myer and John Hardaker for their editorial support.

Finally, I am grateful to my wife, Anita Kaur Jutley, for her tireless support in all aspects, and I apologise to all those who I may have forgotten to thank.

1 **What is fitness?**

We frequently use such expressions as *fitness*, *training* and *body conditioning*, yet many would be hard put to define their exact meanings. Each relates to a state of body and mind and spans a wide range of ability, with top athletes (including top motorsport drivers) at the high end.

There are two important points to note about fitness. First, fitness can be measured. There are components to fitness (most easily remembered as the Ss of fitness – stamina, strength, suppleness, speed, skill and spirit) and by periodic measuring of their levels we can see whether we are making any progress. Second, fitness is sport-specific. For example, although Olympic weightlifters are extremely fit athletes, most would have difficulty running a marathon. The expected contribution of each component and the training time dedicated to it depends on the type of sport and the level of competition. There is, however, some degree of compensation between the components – an experienced squash player might use his or her *skill* to overcome younger opponents of greater *stamina*.

The components of fitness

- *Stamina*. Arguably the most important component in any sport is stamina. In motorsport this component allows the competitor to perform prolonged sub-maximal activity without fatigue. Stamina should certainly never be ignored in any training programme. Also known as aerobic endurance, this

component dictates for how long your body can undertake continuous physical work without tiring.
- *Strength*. This component refers to the maximum force generated by the muscle against a resistance. Hence, strength training is often referred to as resistance training.
- *Speed and suppleness*. Speed and suppleness are also important elements – speed referring to the rapidity of movement of the body, including the reaction time, and suppleness to the range of movement that the joints are capable of. Absolute speed is a priority for track runners and in any sport where short and repeated sprints are necessary. In motorsport, however, it is of lesser importance. Suppleness (or flexibility), on the other hand, is often an underrated component. It was her suppleness that saved the life of Louise Aitken-Walker, 1990 FIA Ladies World Rally Champion, when her car plummeted down a 150-foot cliff during the Portugal WRC Rally and came to rest upside down and underwater in a 20-foot deep river. She managed to extricate herself from the cockpit and roll cage and swim to the surface; something she would not have been able to do had she not been supple.
- *Skill*. Skill and co-ordination are interchangeable and specific to the task. They refer to the smooth and accurate flow of movement as a task is undertaken.

Mr Fitness, Michael Schumacher, shows off his versatility with some fancy footwork with a football.

14

Pasi Hagstrom suffering from heat exhaustion during the 2001 Acropolis Rally. Some drivers consume up to 12 litres of fluid a day to prevent such a problem. (Maurice Selden, Martin Holmes Rallying)

- *Spirit.* If the mind is ill-prepared the body will perform poorly. This often underrated component of fitness refers to the valuable input of psychology in any sport.

Fitness in motorsport

There is no doubt that most current top motorsport drivers are high-level athletes. Ask any trainer looking after the big-name competitors and he or she will tell you of the long months spent working on the various components of fitness. Bernie Shrosbree is well known amongst motorsport training circles. Employed by the Renault Formula 1 team as their Human Performance Manager, this former member of the Special Forces and triathlete is no stranger to physical and mental fitness. As a trainer of Jenson Button and

This chart shows the relative importance of the major components of fitness in motorsport competitors. Skill has not been included as it is not the purpose of this book to teach the reader how to drive a car.

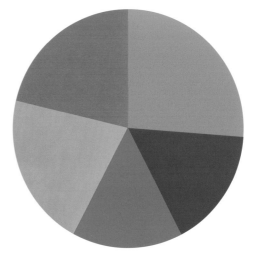

strength
speed
suppleness
stamina
spirit

Jarno Trulli, amongst other prominent personalities such as 1995 FIA World Rally Champion Colin McRae, Bernie explains:

> Although the various forms of motorsport require different specifics of fitness, for instance, strong neck and shoulders in F1 and strong lumbar region and forearms in rallying, there is a need for all drivers to have a base level of aerobic and strength conditioning on which to build these specific aspects.

Certain components of fitness are given more emphasis when it comes to motorsport-specific training. Apart from skill, which may be natural or developed, upper body strength is probably the most crucial component for motorsport competitors. Not only do drivers constantly battle with the steering wheel, often without the luxury of powered steering, they are also subjected to g-forces that place massive strains on their necks and upper bodies. In Formula 1 racing, g-forces as high as 4g have been reported during some of the corners at famous tracks. To subject untrained neck muscles to such forces could result in permanent damage.

Marcus Gronholm, the 2000 and 2002 World Rally Champion and Peugeot driver, receives on-the-spot attention from medical staff during a round. Rallying places massive stresses on the neck owing to g-forces encountered during acceleration and braking. (Maurice Selden, Martin Holmes Rallying)

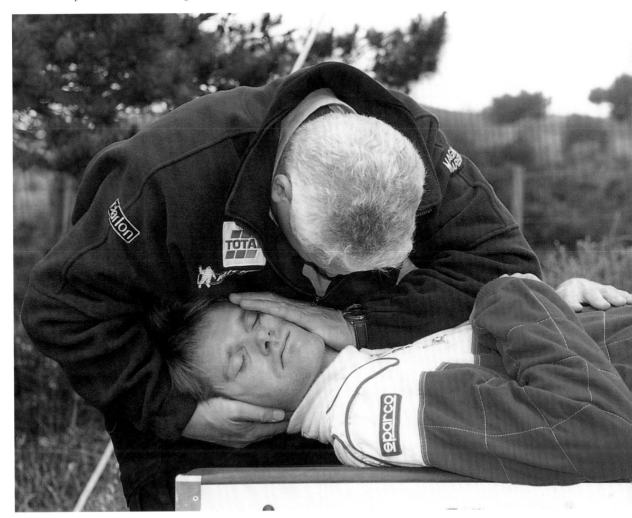

2 Before you
start training

There are two routines that it is essential to incorporate into your every training programme or else you could end up with damage to your body. These are *warming up* and *cooling down*. Ignore these two important principles at your peril!

Warming up

A warm-up means exactly what it says. Very simply it is a routine designed to condition your muscles for the work that is about to follow. It increases the blood flow to your muscles and raises your muscle working temperatures. This makes the tissues, like your tendons (which join muscles to bone) and ligaments (which join bone to bone) more flexible and guards them against strain and injury. An adequate warm-up also raises your breathing and heart rate and there is also evidence that a warm-up prevents irregular heartbeats as the heart is stressed less suddenly.

- Start gently and work your whole body so you feel warm. Suggested routines include brisk walking and/or light jogging. As a guide, if you work up a light sweat during the warm-up you are doing well. Avoid any explosive and sudden movements.
- Use warm-up techniques that are going to be replicated during your exercises. For example, do some flat terrain cycling for a mile or so if you are planning on a cycle ride. A brisk walk is a good start for running. In the gym, 5 to 15 minutes on the cycle machine at low resistance is an excellent routine.

- DO NOT think that stretching is a replacement for warming up. It is an excellent adjunct to warm-up but certainly not a replacement. Although you should try a whole-body stretch beforehand, stretch the muscles and joints that you are likely to be using AFTER the warm up.
- AVOID warming up more than 30 minutes before undertaking the training. A time lag of any longer will mean that your muscles will have cooled down considerably.

Cooling down

Just as important as easing into your exercise routine is easing out of it at the end. The benefits are several, yet a cool-down is largely ignored by many athletes. Remember that your body must adapt to its usual routine after the strenuous workout. It needs to expel all the waste products like lactic acid from the muscles. It must prevent pooling of blood in places that no longer require high flow. Your heart must slowly regain its normal working rate.

A cool-down may be done by gradually reducing intensity of the exercise performed. If on a bike ride, finish off by doing a few miles on the flat. On the gym machine, crank down the level of your training as you come to the end of your session. A whole body stretch is another excellent way of cooling down. There is some evidence that it prevents muscular soreness and stiffness. Other adjuncts to cooling down include the use of massage, hot baths and Jacuzzis.

Just as important as warming up before training is cooling down afterwards, and here Jenson Button enjoys a massage to help in the cooling down process.

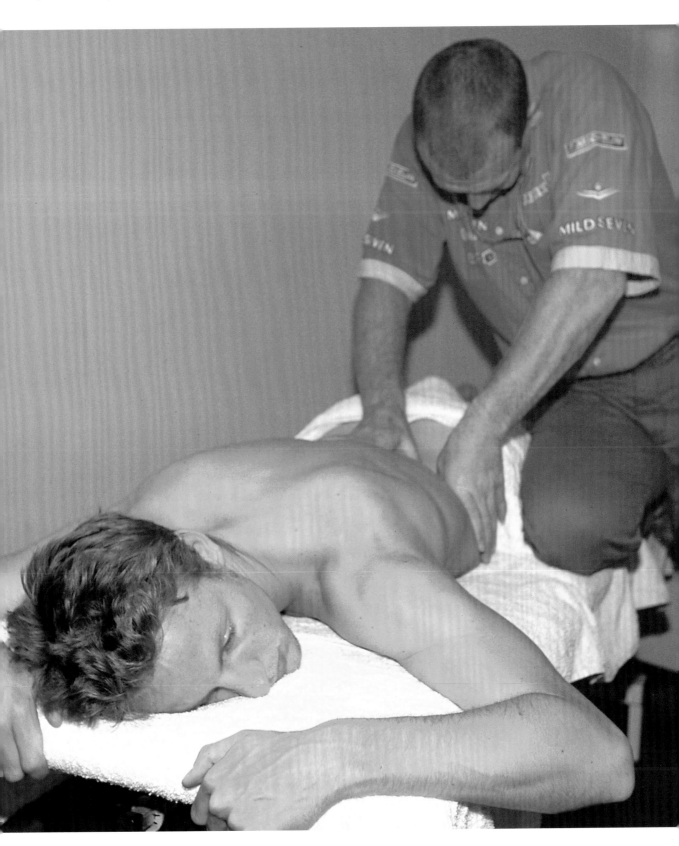

③ Stamina

Colin McRae working on his endurance in a purpose-built gym at his home. (Colin McMaster/McKlein)

The relationship between aerobic and anaerobic metabolism with lactate and the onset of fatigue. As exercise intensity rises and oxygen demand outstrips supply the muscles switch to anaerobic metabolism. This point, shown by the dotted line, is known as the anaerobic threshold.

To perform any exercise your muscles must be supplied with energy. This energy comes from the breakdown of fat and carbohydrate, a process which requires oxygen and is known as *aerobic metabolism*. Your capacity for continuing strenuous activity for any length of time, or your stamina, is therefore largely dependent upon how well your lungs and cardiovascular system work. As exercise intensifies, oxygen demand increases proportionally, and to meet that demand your lungs are called upon to breathe more heavily and your heart to pump more rapidly to get the extra oxygen into the bloodstream and delivered as quickly as possible to the muscles you are using. How effectively this challenge is met is a measure of your fitness, but sooner or later there comes a time when the oxygen supply cannot keep up with the working demands

of the muscles and you become fatigued or exhausted.

As oxygen demand begins to outpace supply, your muscles will start to switch to *anaerobic metabolism* (burning the fuel without oxygen). With anaerobic metabolism your muscles will operate about 19 times less efficiently than with aerobic metabolism and there will also be a more rapid build-up of *lactic acid* (lactate) which adversely affects muscle function and causes that unpleasant burning sensation.

Training will bring about changes in your muscles at cellular level and can improve both your aerobic and anaerobic capacity.

Aerobic endurance is as important in motorsport as it is in any other sport. During competition drivers' upper body muscles especially are constantly working to keep their cars on the road. In endurance racing it may be several hours before drivers' muscles are allowed to rest, and during this time they will also be fighting the on-going battle against dehydration in a high temperature environment. If not conditioned beforehand, their working muscles will become prematurely fatigued by a rapid accumulation of lactic acid. The West McLaren Mercedes Formula 1 team, for one, recognises this and regularly conducts aerobic fitness tests to evaluate their drivers' anaerobic thresholds. The following section shows how you can do the same tests on yourself.

The need for training to build up stamina is borne out by the results of research work conducted some years ago with Formula 1 and production car racing drivers. Jean-Louis Schlesser was found to have recorded a heart rate of up to 195 beats per minute in a production car race,

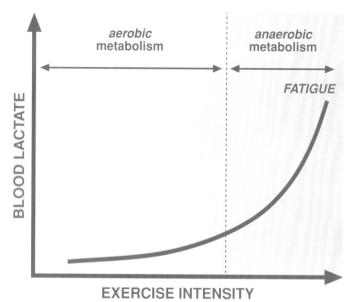

and during a first session at Le Mans, Didier Pironi clearly showed a marked variation in heart rate between straights and corners. His heart rates were generally higher during cornering. More recently Renault conducted their own research into this during Formula 1 testing at Valencia and Barcelona, with similar results. The high heart rates that have been recorded are close to the limits of human tolerance and can only be sustained by those who are physically fit. Anyone in poor condition could suffer a heart attack if subjected to such high pulse rates.

Measuring aerobic fitness – the VO$_2$max concept

Aerobic fitness relates to the body's highest rate of oxygen consumption. It is referred to in sports fitness circles as the maximum oxygen uptake or *VO$_2$max*. To provide a more accurate measure, VO$_2$max is calculated as the amount of oxygen taken up per kilogram of body weight per minute (ml/kg/min). The higher your VO$_2$max the fitter you are, although remember that values are determined by age, sex, height and weight as well as level of fitness.

Many gyms will have qualified instructors to measure your VO$_2$max using a variety of methods. The most accurate method involves wearing a mask or mouthpiece to collect expired air whilst exercising at increasing intensity. This method is, however, usually restricted to research laboratories, but the alternatives given below have been shown to correlate well with the more sophisticated tests.

The one-mile walking test

Use this test if you have not been training. To calculate your VO$_2$max the figures you need are your weight in lbs, your age, the time you take to do the walk to the nearest 1/100th minute and your heart rate at the end of it. The formula is:

VO$_2$max = 132.853 – (0.0769 x weight in lbs) – (0.3877 x age in years) + (6.315 x1 for male, 0 for female) – (3.2649 x time) – (0.1565 x heart rate at end of test)

Let's consider Jim, an amateur rally driver aged 35, weighing 85kg (187lb). He completes the course in 13 minutes 20 seconds (13.33min) and has a heart rate of 145 at the end. His VO$_2$max is then:

132.853 – (0.0769 x 187) – (0.3877 x 35) + (6.315 x1) – (3.2649 x 13.33) – (0.1565 x 145) = 45ml/kg/min

Remember to measure out a mile and *walk* the course as fast as possible.

The 1.5 mile running test

This is also known as the Balke test. Only attempt this test if you have been training beforehand and have a reasonable fitness level. Otherwise seek medical advice.

Measure out 1.5 miles and run the distance as quickly as possible. Then use the table to estimate your VO$_2$max.

VO$_2$max testing may also be performed using treadmills and static bicycles but these require special equipment usually found only in laboratories and some gyms.

Improving stamina – the training heart rate concept

It's clear that to improve your stamina you need to undertake exercise of a sufficiently high intensity, and that intensity is measured by your heart rate.

VO$_2$max values in active people and elite athletes. The values generally peak in the third decade. With each decade the VO$_2$max declines by up to 10% depending upon the level of activity.

VO$_2$max values in ml/kg/min		
	Men	**Women**
Active	50-65	35-50
Elite athletes	65-90	55-70

Unless you have a heart problem, generally the lower your resting heart rate (pulse) the fitter you are. The method described is accurate when measuring progress in training and is used regularly by many professional athletes. Most individuals have a resting rate of between 60 and 90. With regular exercise your resting rate will drop as your heart becomes more efficient. Top marathon runners and some Formula 1 drivers have resting heart rates in the 30s and 40s!

To best take your resting rate, do it while lying still in bed having woken from a good night's sleep. This time is preferable as you are least likely to be subject to any influence from muscular activity or from the intake of stimulants such as caffeine in coffee or tea. The pulse at the wrist is ideal for measurement, or the carotid artery may also be used as described in detail in the emergency care chapter. Put your finger on your pulse and count the pulses over a minute. An easier way is to use a heart-rate monitor. These can be bought in most sports outlets.

Everyone should know their maximum heart rate. This number is important as it allows training intensity to be calculated. The most commonly used method for arriving at a rough estimate of your maximum heart rate is to subtract your age from 220. Jim, the amateur driver who is 35 years of age, should have a maximum heart rate of 220 − 35 = 185 beats per minute.

Your training zone

Most experts recommend that to gain any benefit from exercise you should train within a particular training zone, usually between 50% to 85% of your maximum heart rate. This means that Jim would have a training zone minimum of 185 x 0.50 = 93 beats per minute, and a maximum of 185 x 0.85 = 157 beats per minute.

Towards the higher end of your training zone your body tends to be close to its anaerobic threshold.

Time (min:sec)	Estimated VO₂max (ml/kg/min)	Fitness Level
Under 7:30	75	
7:31– 8:00	72	
8:01– 8:30	67	HIGH
8:31– 9:00	62	
9:01– 9:30	58	
9:31–10:00	55	GOOD
10:01–10:30	49	
10:31–11:00	46	AVERAGE
11:01–11:30	44	
11:31–12:00	41	
12:01–12:30	39	
12:31–13:00	37	FAIR
13:01–13:30	36	
13:31–14:00	33	
14:01–14:30	31	
14:31–15:00	30	LOW

The Karvonen formula

As mentioned above, the '220 minus your age' method of establishing maximum heart rate is not particularly exact. A more accurate method is to use the Karvonen formula which takes into account your resting heart rate. It requires slightly more maths but is easy enough to work out. The steps are as follows:

1 Take away your age from 220.
2 Take away your resting heart rate from that value.
3 To work out the lower end of your training zone, multiply the result of Step 2 by 50% and add you resting pulse to it.
4 To work out the upper end of your training zone, multiply the result of Step 2 by 85% and add you resting pulse to it.

For example, Jim has a resting heart rate of 80 beats per minute. According to the Karvonen formula his maximum heart rate should be 169, worked out as follows:

Estimation of VO₂max using the 1.5 mile running test. This is based on a population of males ages 20–29 years. By moving up one category, the values for females may be obtained. (Used with permission from Fitness For Sport by Rex Hazeldine, Crowood Press.)

23

1　$220 - 35 = 185$
2　$185 - 80 = 105$
3　$105 \times 0.5 = 53; 53 + 80 = 133$
　　(minimum training heart rate)
4　$105 \times 0.85 = 89; 89 + 80 = 169$
　　(maximum training heart rate)

Why measure heart rates?

To some, measuring and calculating heart rates may sound tedious. However, it has been shown to be of great benefit when assessing progress during training. For example, you may find that Level 2 on the gym machine initially pushed your heart rate to 150. After a month the same level only raises it to 130. This shows a definite and measurable increase in stamina. Many elite athletes also use heart rate monitoring to assess whether they have recovered from heavy workouts. If, first thing in the morning, their heart rate is higher than usual, it is likely that they have not recovered from their previous workout.

Another good indicator of improvement in fitness is the time it takes for your heart rate to recover to lower levels. Next time you are in the gym take your pulse rate as soon as you complete your training session, and take it again after a minute. Generally, the faster the drop the fitter you are.

Designing an aerobic exercise plan

Naturally, exercise plans are tailored to suit needs. These might be to burn fat, to lose weight, to gain weight, to build strength or to improve fitness and restore a feeling of well-being. Our aim here is to improve your fitness level, or in other words to improve your VO_2 max and lower your resting heart rate. Most people undertake this level of training in response to a challenge, such as a marathon, and it requires a fair amount of dedication to see things through.

The secret is to *gradually* build up the intensity and duration of your regime. It is important not to go at it too strongly and run the risk of injuring yourself early in the programme. Start off with three sessions a week with at least a full day's rest between sessions. Make each session variable in length and intensity. For example, go on for up to an hour at the lower end of your training zone. On other days go for 40-minute sessions at around 85% of your maximum heart rate. As your fitness improves, aim for five sessions a week. Increase the duration of the training by around 10% every week. The intensity of your training will change automatically as you find it progressively easier to perform the same task.

A weight-loss programme generally requires longer workouts so the body burns fat preferentially. As a guide, 45–60min workouts are probably sufficient at around 50–70% maximum heart rate. Try to work out regularly at this low intensity. If you combine the exercises with the weight loss tips given later in this book you will be doing well.

Maximising training

As your fitness improves you can start to modify your training programme to include the following with a view to maximising the benefits.

The changes in heart rate in Gilles Villeneuve during a training session at Monaco. This reflects the extraordinary aerobic fitness in the legendary racing driver. (Courtesy: Prof Sid Watkins)

The Renault F1 drivers, Jenson Button, Jarno Trulli and Fernando Alonso, during their driver training programme in Kenya before the start of the 2002 season. The drivers are seen combining cross-terrain trekking and cycling to maximise their endurance.
(Renault F1)

Fartlek

Swedish for 'speed play', this training method allows you to vary the pace and intensity of your programme at random and in a carefree manner. For example, when jogging decide to sprint for five seconds at every third telegraph pole and slow to a fast walk at every fifth for 100 yards.

Interval training

A very popular method of aerobic training where you combine short, intense spurts of exercise with short periods of recovery at lower intensity exercise. The spurts may last as little as 15 seconds. Many gym treadmills, cycle machines, rowing machines and cross-trainers now offer interval training as a standard programme. The advantage of interval training is that it progressively builds up aerobic capacity in the muscles by taking them close to their fatigue limit.

Uphill and cross terrain

Walking slowly up a steep hill requires as much energy as running on the flat. Walking on sand requires twice as much as doing the same on hard ground.

Circuit training

A widely used method to improve aerobic and muscular endurance as well as speed. It involves setting up a circuit of aerobic and muscular exercises that may be specific to the sport. Details of motorsport specific circuit training appear later in the book.

When to take a break

Just as important as training hard is knowing when to stop. The balance is right if you combine various intensities of workouts in a typical week. If you experience the following signs then you have probably overdone it:

- You always feel tired and sore
- You are prone to colds
- You sleep poorly
- Your concentration span is short
- You are easily irritated.

What top drivers do

West McLaren Mercedes Formula 1 Team

The McLaren facility at Woking has a Human Performance Laboratory designed to improve and measure the fitness of their drivers. The VO_2 max, anaerobic threshold and resting heart rates are all assessed at regular intervals during the year. The lab is run by Jerry Powell, head of physiology.

Renault F1 team

At Renault F1's Human Performance Centre, drivers are assessed regularly throughout the year to ensure that high fitness standards are maintained. Tests include lactate threshold, VO_2 max, motor reaction and fatigue reaction times, muscular endurance and strength. Programmes are personally tailored to ensure drivers work on areas which need attention and not just what they enjoy doing. For instance, Jenson Button will favour different sessions from Jarno Trulli but both have to work on areas identified in testing as needing improvement.

Jim Moodie

To maintain and improve stamina Jim subjects himself to a fairly punishing routine in the gym, especially during winter months before the race season. Jim does not enjoy running and maintains 80% of his maximum heart rate on the cross-trainer for up to 30 minutes before pushing himself to 100% for five minutes at the end of the routine. This should only be attempted by those who are exceptionally fit and capable of withstanding the stresses of the exercise.

Colin McRae enjoys the outdoors and would rather be mountain biking in the hills as he is here with his younger brother and Mitsubishi World Rally Team driver, Alister. (Colin McMaster/McKlein)

27

4 Strength

Strength is one of the most important components of fitness for the motorsport competitor, and this chapter gives specific advice on how to improve upper body strength, a crucial part of a driver's training programme.

Put simply, your strength is the maximum force that you can exert against a resistance. Hence, strength training is often referred to as *resistance training*.

There are essentially two types of strength, *isotonic* and *isometric*. Isotonic (*iso* = equal and *tonic* = tone) strength is also known as dynamic strength and relates to the normal contraction of muscles as body parts are moved, for example, to lift a heavy weight off the ground. Isometric (*iso* = equal and *metric* = length) strength is sometimes referred to as static strength and relates to muscular pressure without contraction. Here the muscle exerts a pushing force such as pressing straight-armed against a solid wall.

Forces of up to 4g or 5g are not uncommon during braking and cornering at motorsport events. Considering that the combined weight of an average head and helmet is around 4kg (about 9lb), this means the neck muscles must support up to 20kg (44lb) during such manoeuvres. A typical track event lasts over 50 laps, each with around 12 corners, in heat and humidity that drains away the energy of any driver. To make matters even worse, if the race is on a clockwise circuit, the muscles on the right side of the neck will take more of a hammering than those on the left.

Upper body strength is also important when it comes to the physical effort of driving a race or rally car. The simple fact is that weak muscles will quickly tire and prevent a driver from maintaining peak performance.

Jarno Trulli working his upper body during driver training in Kenya before the 2002 season. (Renault F1)

Bernie Shrosbree, Human Performance Manager at Renault F1, says:

A man off the street who considers himself very fit would only last a few laps of a typical Formula 1 race circuit. The next day he would struggle to even lift his head off the pillow. That's how tough the g-forces are on your neck.

Measuring muscle strength

Your *isotonic* or dynamic strength can be established by seeing how heavy a weight you can lift. Alternatively you can see how much you can lift if you were to do two or more repetitions. This gives you a baseline against which you can measure your progress. There is a variety of exercises to choose from, for example a biceps curl or a bench press (see later), as your baseline workout. You will know you are making progress when you have to increase the weight you are lifting to tire your muscles. Another method, not requiring weights, is to count the number of non-stop press-ups you can do.

Isometric or static strength testing can be judged by the lateral hang test. Hang off a horizontal beam with your feet off the ground and hold the position for as long as possible, as shown in *Fig. 1*.

Knowing the lingo

For benefit, muscles must be exposed to *overload*. They then get bigger and stronger, a process known as *hypertrophy*. The number of times you perform an exercise without stopping is known as the *repetitions*, or '*reps*' as some like to call them. Although there is no optimum number of repetitions, research has shown

Know your upper body muscles. (Line drawings: Agarwal. Photos: Mike Gibbon, MVG Photographic)

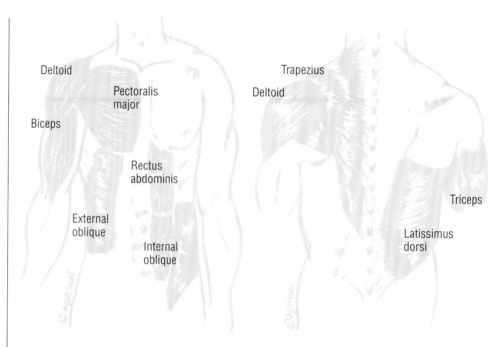

Deltoid

Pectoralis major

Biceps

Rectus abdominis

External oblique

Internal oblique

Trapezius

Deltoid

Triceps

Latissimus dorsi

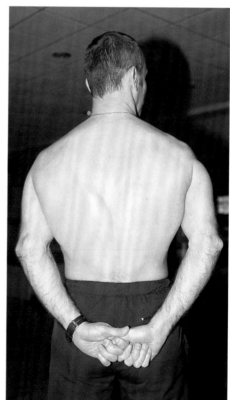

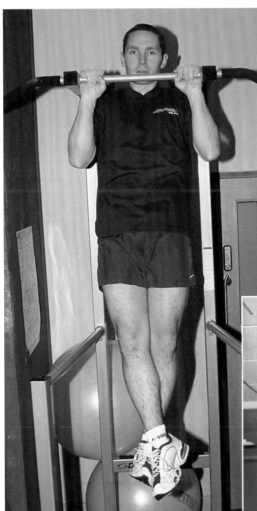

Fig. 1. The lateral hang test which tests static or isometric strength. Make sure that you keep still when doing the test. (Mike Gibbon, MVG Photographic)

that the weight you lift must be sufficient to allow a maximum of ten repetitions to be undertaken.

A *set* is a number of repetitions. Again, many recommend a start of just one set with a progressive build-up to three as strength develops.

Resistance is the load that you are working against. It may simply be in weight measures such as kilograms or a scale, for example one to ten.

Progressive muscular or *resistance training* is when you choose a set number of repetitions, usually ten, and when more repetitions are possible, you simply increase the load to bring the repetition number back down.

How much to do

When starting a strength training programme, decide what you want to achieve. Chart your performance in a diary and regularly measure your muscles on a three-week basis. Try to workout at least three to five times a week as this has been shown to be more effective. A good start is 3 x 10 repetitions every other day. As a general rule, a lower number of repetitions at higher loads builds strength. A high repetition at lower loads leads to

endurance. Try to mix both if you can.

Remember that working with heavy weights can be dangerous. Safety is always a priority. Be sensible and start with low weights, and make sure that you rest for about a minute between sets and at least two days between particularly heavy workouts to allow your muscles to recover. Try to alternate muscle groups so the same muscles are not always stressed.

Actually, you don't have to use free weights or machines for strength or resistance training. Your body is an excellent form of resistance.

Motorsport-specific strength training

Press-ups

An excellent exercise that works many upper body muscles if done correctly (see *Fig. 2*). Men should attempt press-ups whilst keeping their body rigid throughout the entire manoeuvre and their knees off the ground. Women should perform the exercise pivoting on their knees with their feet off the ground. To increase the intensity try to push off explosively and clap your hands. The very fit can do press-ups with one arm.

A member of the public, even if very fit, would only last a few laps of a typical F1 race. (Sporting Pictures UK)

Fig. 2. Press-ups done correctly. (Mike Gibbon, MVG Photographic)

Fig. 3. The recommended method for performing dips. (Mike Gibbon, MVG Photographic)

Dips

Done with the help of a low bench or chair, this exercise works the triceps, pectorals and latissimus dorsi muscles (see *Fig. 3*). Make sure that your support does not move during the exercise. For maximum effectiveness keep your legs straight and lower yourself until your buttocks touch the ground. Then return until your arms are straight. For advanced training, use a partner to apply downward pressure as you perform the exercise.

Chin-ups

A horizontal beam can be used either with an overgrasp or undergrasp grip. Make sure that you work from your arms fully straight to fully bent at the elbows if possible. If these chin-ups are a problem, try them with your feet on the ground (see *Fig. 4*). For an advanced workout try bending your knees in front of your chest.

Fig. 4. Chin-ups with the feet on the ground. These are useful if the proper method proves difficult. (Mike Gibbon, MVG Photographic)

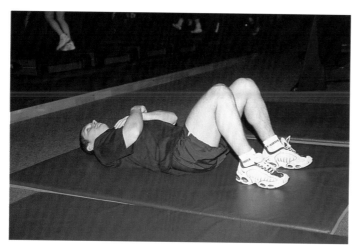

Abdominal work

Abdominal muscles are crucial to the stability of the back and must never be ignored during training. A well-tested method of increasing muscular strength of the abdominal wall is to perform sit-ups. Lie on your back with your knees bent. Cross your arms across your chest and try not to anchor your feet if at all possible (see *Fig. 5*). Curl your body to a half-sitting position. To make it easier you can place your arms alongside your body. To make it more advanced, bend your knees to 90°. To work your internal and external obliques, twist your body so that you (attempt to) touch the opposite knee to your elbow keeping your shoulders off the ground.

Fig. 5. Abdominal curls with the arms crossed in front of the chest. (Mike Gibbon, MVG Photographic)

Back work

In motorsport it is important that your back muscles are kept strong as they will be subjected to stresses, strains, jolts and jarring well outside everyday tolerances. In fact, research has shown that about half of all Formula 1 drivers suffer, or have suffered, from back ailments. Moreover, Carlos Sainz, twice FIA World Rally Champion, knows only too well the consequences of a bad back during an event. He works regularly in the gym to keep his back muscles strong. Although careful stretching is a great way of maintaining suppleness (see Chapter 5) it is important that the muscles are kept strengthened as well.

Trunk and leg lifts, as shown in *Fig. 6* and *Fig. 7* are good strengthening exercises. Make sure that you do not overdo the extensions.

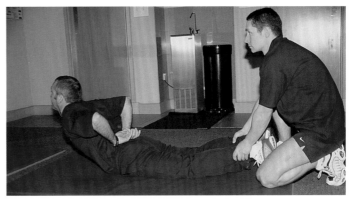

Fig. 6. Trunk lift with the feet stabilised. (Mike Gibbon, MVG Photographic)

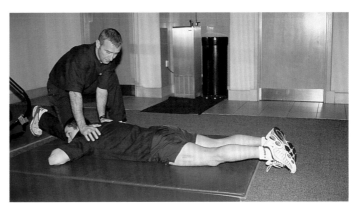

Fig. 7. Leg lifts are best done with the help of a partner who holds the upper body down. (Mike Gibbon, MVG Photographic)

Use of weights or machines

Most gyms provide free weights and machines for strength training. Again, safety is the priority here. Get the gym staff to show you the recommended methods of using the weights and machines. It is good practice to breathe in when making the effort and breathe out when releasing the tension.

As a general guide, some of the essential exercises for upper body strength are as follows:

The biceps curl is possibly the most commonly performed exercise for the biceps muscles. Fig. 8 shows the starting and finishing positions. Make sure that your arms are fully straight when lowering them and bent when raising the bar so that it touches your chest. Your elbows must also be kept stationary next to your body. (Mike Gibbon, MVG Photographic)

Fig. 9. Triceps extension. Use a dumb bell for this with the weight positioned behind your head. Straighten your arm, at the same time stabilising your elbow with your other hand. (Mike Gibbon, MVG Photographic)

Fig. 10. Military press. Raise the bar to the top of your chest to begin with. Straighten out your arms over your head to perform the military press. (Mike Gibbon, MVG Photographic)

Military press

This workout is great for the arms and shoulder muscles. Keep your feet about shoulder width apart to provide a stable platform. The exercise can be performed while sitting (see *Fig. 10*).

Fig. 11. The bench press, which is most effectively performed with the arms fully straight or bent to take the bar to the chest. (Mike Gibbon, MVG Photographic)

Bench press

This exercise is essential to develop the shoulders, arms and chest (see *Fig. 11*). It also requires a high degree of safety, with partners present to lift the weight off when needed.

Latissimus pull down

The latissimus muscle is what provides the V-shaped torso that musclemen have. The machine for performing the exercise is very popular and may be found in most gyms with instructions for its use (see *Fig. 12*).

What top drivers do

Iain McPherson

Upper body strength is important for Super Sport competition but Iain recognises that too bulky and muscular a body may also be a hindrance. He prefers to do body resistance work and concentrates largely on press-ups and pull-ups.

Fig. 12. Latissimus pull down. The exercise may be performed either by kneeling or sitting on a bench. Bring the bar to the top of your chest in a smooth and controlled motion. (Mike Gibbon, MVG Photographic)

Colin McRae working his biceps using bar bells. These weights are useful alternatives to the longer straight bar and are readily available in most sports outlets. (Colin McMaster/ McKlein)

41

5 **Suppleness**

Suppleness, also known as flexibility, is the range of movement you have in your joints and the ease with which you can bend without causing damage to muscles, tendons and ligaments. Levels of suppleness vary widely between individuals, but the important thing is that you can develop and improve your flexibility with appropriate training. Flexibility training is indeed the cornerstone of any sportsperson's fitness programme, although traditionally many motorsport competitors have not seen it as a priority. Strength and stamina are certainly the more obvious physical requirements for motorsport drivers, but these qualities cannot be optimised without specific flexibility training, and there is no doubt that it should be an integral component in your preparation for, and recovery from, races and rallies at any level.

This chapter shows why flexibility is important to you as a motorsport driver, and how you can improve your own flexibility.

Bernie Shrosbree, Human Performance Manager for Renault F1 says:

> Flexibility is crucial, for greater ranges of movement promote strength and help prevent injury in impacts such as those sustained in crashes. This is because, when the body is subjected to high impact forces and limbs and body segments are moved around at high velocity, a greater range of movement around each joint will reduce the likelihood of muscle and ligament damage.

So, by developing your flexibility you will become less vulnerable to injury, and should you sustain an injury your recovery time will be that much quicker.

A simple way to find out how flexible you are is to bend forward with your knees straight and see if you can touch your toes. If you can do this easily you are supple, and if you can go further and place your hands flat on the ground you are very supple. Admittedly this tests only the flexibility of your lower back and rear thighs but it's a good indicator of your general suppleness, and it's probably not necessary to check the mobility of all your joints to find out how much work you need to do on this aspect of fitness. However, if you want to extend your assessment, your local fitness centre will be able to take you through a few simple flexibility tests to see where you stand. Some sophisticated gyms may have goniometers, which measure angles, to assess your suppleness.

Getting more flexible

Flexibility training can be divided into two main components – general warm-up and specific stretching. Also, yoga and massage, although beyond the scope of this book, are helpful in becoming supple and maintaining suppleness, and are well worth consideration as part of an overall fitness routine.

General warm-up

A good warm-up is important before both training and competing as it gets your heart and other muscles up to a point where they can function most efficiently. It will increase the blood flow to your muscles, thereby enhancing the supply of oxygen and removing accumulated lactic acid and other waste products, and it will of course lead to a slight increase in temperature of the body tissues involved in the exercise, thus improving their elasticity.

Jim Moodie, seven-times winner of the Isle of Man TT, keeps supple by exercising in the gym. (Mike Gibbon, MVG Photographic)

9 Weight loss in motorsport   **10** Motorsport-specific circuit training   **11** The event   **12** Emergency care in motorsp

1 What is fitn

As well as the physical benefits, a warm-up can increase the level of arousal to its optimal point, giving you time to focus on and rehearse the race or rally course and its various twists and turns. The psychological aspects of competitive driving are covered in more depth in Chapter 7.

The way you warm up will depend on individual preference and the facilities available. It can be *active* through either a gentle jog or cycle ride, or *passive* with the use of a hot shower or sauna. Passive warm-up is particularly useful if you are recovering from a previous injury.

Spend between 10 to 15 minutes doing a general warm-up. *Do not rush it!* It should be intense enough to cause mild sweating but not vigorous enough to tire you for the training or the event. Remember that the specific muscle stretching to come can be performed more effectively when the tissues are warmed.

It seems obvious, but always be prepared for the conditions you are likely to find yourself in. If you are on a cold, windswept hillside awaiting the start of your event, you should wear appropriate clothing to keep yourself warm and dry. Stay on the move and time your warm-up and stretching so that you don't cool off before your start time.

Specific stretching

Motorsport-specific stretching should concentrate on the neck, shoulders and arms – the parts of the body which will be worked hardest in the cockpit – and on the back and trunk muscles as driving a race or rally car places significant strain on this area, particularly the lumbar region (lower back).

The following exercises are designed for use before starting an event, and when rallying they can also be used between stages while both you and the car take a pit stop to refuel. After each gruelling stage your muscles and joints will be stiff and possibly painful, and full advantage should be taken of the break to 'loosen-off' and allow your body to regain its optimum performance.

Of the several approaches to stretching, the one most appropriate to motorsport, and as it happens the simplest, is *static stretching*. This is a style of stretching familiar to most people. It involves bending a limb to the point where tightness is felt as the tissues are stretched and then holding the posture for up to 30 seconds, after which time it can be released. The nerve endings in your tendons sense the stretch and send a message to your muscles to relax, increasing flexibility. It is, of course, important not to exert excessive strain on your tissues.

So what odd positions will you need to put your body in so you can drive better? Well, here are a few examples of stretching exercises that you might consider as part of your routine. Remember, if at any stage of these exercises you feel pain it is vital you stop immediately.

Neck

This exercise can be performed standing or sitting. Keeping your back straight, place your left hand above your right ear, gently stretching your neck to the left, at the same time pulling your right shoulder downwards (see *Fig. 1*). This can be aided by holding on to a fixed object. Care should be taken when putting the power into the shoulder stretch to protect the neck. The exercise should then be repeated on the other side. To adjust the point of stretch, the head can be flexed forwards or extended backwards.

Fig. 1. Stretching the neck muscles, which can take a fair amount of battering during most motorsport events … (Mike Gibbon, MVG Photographic)

… particularly when cornering like this! (Sporting Pictures UK)

Fig. 2. Stretching the upper or thoracic spine. (Mike Gibbon, MVG Photographic)

Back and trunk

The upper or thoracic part of the spine is easily stretched by kneeling down on all fours, sitting back on your ankles and reaching your hands forward as in *Fig. 2*. Hold this position for more than 30 seconds for maximum benefit.

Lower back flexion can be achieved by lying on your back, drawing your knees up to your chest, and maintaining the posture using your arms (see *Fig. 3*). Flexing your neck forward will increase the stretch on your spinal muscles.

Extension of the lower back is especially useful in releasing the strain and pressure on the back resulting from prolonged sitting. Lying on your front, push up from the *press-up* position. Do not force the posture as this can cause injury. Pause at the top of the movement, return to the starting position, and repeat in a slow rhythmical manner (see *Fig. 4*). As well as the spine you will feel the central abdominal muscles stretched during this exercise.

Fig. 3. Stretching the lower or lumbar spine. (Mike Gibbon, MVG Photographic)

Fig. 4. Extending the back. (Mike Gibbon, MVG Photographic)

Fig. 5. Stretching the abdominal muscles. (Mike Gibbon, MVG Photographic)

The lateral abdominal muscles are stretched by standing with feet shoulder width apart to maintain balance (see *Fig. 5*). Keeping your head up and back straight, arms raised, rotate alternately left to right. The exercise can also be done in the sitting position, holding a stick to maintain the posture. (see *Fig. 6*).

Fig. 6. Stretching the abdominal muscles while sitting, using a stick to maintain posture. (Mike Gibbon, MVG Photographic)

Shoulders

Kneeling down, place your hands on your lower back or buttocks. Attempt to draw your elbows together, feeling the stretch around the muscles of the shoulder girdle (see *Fig. 7*).

The front of your shoulders and the muscles of your chest are easily stretched by standing in a doorway with your hands on the frame to take your weight, and gently leaning forward, as shown in *Fig. 8*.

Fig. 7. Stretching the muscles of the shoulder girdle. (Mike Gibbon, MVG Photographic)

Fig. 8. Stretching of the front of the chest wall and shoulders exercise. (Mike Gibbon, MVG Photographic)

Gripping the doorframe, or another fixed object, high up, keeping your arms straight and bending your legs to increase the pull on your arms, will stretch your lateral shoulder muscles and your triceps muscles on the back of the upper arm (see Fig. 9).

During each of these exercises the position of your hands can be adjusted to alter the line of pull and therefore the part of the muscles or muscle group stretched.

Fig. 9. By transferring your grip to the top of the doorframe and bending your legs the outer deltoids and triceps are stretched. (Mike Gibbon, MVG Photographic)

Fig. 10. Gently stretching the hamstring muscles. (Mike Gibbon, MVG Photographic)

Legs

The cramped position of a competition car can cause considerable discomfort and tightness, particularly affecting the hamstring muscles on the back of the upper legs. These muscles can easily be stretched by simply sitting on the ground, legs straight in front of you, keeping your head up, gently curling your back and reaching forward towards your toes. You can sit on or use a stool to support one leg at a time to give variety to this exercise, as shown in *Fig. 10*.

Forearms and wrists

Holding a stick in your right hand while supporting your wrist with your left hand, alternately twist your wrist, first palm up then palm down (supination and pronation), to stretch the muscles of your forearm (see *Fig. 11*). Flexion and extension of your wrist can be achieved by alternately holding each of the positions illustrated for 10–20 seconds (see *Fig. 12*).

Fig. 11. The twisting of the wrist joint through its full range of movement, known as pronation and supination, is rather like twisting a screwdriver. (Mike Gibbon, MVG Photographic)

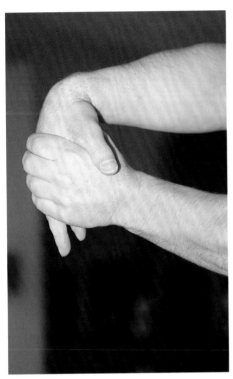

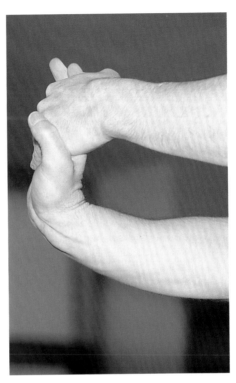

Fig. 12. The flexion and extension of the wrist is performed alternately. (Mike Gibbon, MVG Photographic)

Jim Moodie shows the suppleness that is not uncommon in racers of his standard. (Mike Gibbon, MVG Photographic)

6 Speed

Keeping your car on the track calls for quick reactions, particularly when throwing it round twisty rally stages at night, like this WRC Subaru driver. (Mike Gibbon, MVG Photographic)

The start of a Formula 1 Grand Prix. Not uncommonly the race is lost if the driver fails to secure the lead at the first corner. (Mike Gibbon, MVG Photographic)

Whilst it is obvious that speed of limb movement is important in many sports, particularly in athletics, its value in motorsport may not be immediately clear. But, think about the need for rapid arm action when trying to keep your car or kart under control, and the benefits become more apparent.

In the context of training and fitness, speed relates to the time taken to perform a task. It includes the time taken to react, the *reaction* or *response time* (some call it your *reflexes*) and the time taken to move your body through the specific task, the *movement time*.

Clearly, a faster reaction time to the lights on the starting grid of a track race will determine who gets to the first corner in the lead. Not uncommonly this also determines who wins the race. Reaction time is a function of both your state of mind (psychology) and your body (physiology). Mentally alert and prepared drivers have a shorter response time, as do those who have been practising. The psychology is discussed later in the book. This chapter provides guidance on how to improve your reaction and movement time.

In motorsport, driver response time has also got its safety implications. Your ability to avoid an unexpected rock or an unwary spectator who wanders on to a rally stage is a function of your reaction and movement time.

Bernie Shrosbree feels agility is often underrated in motorsport. He uses the Batak Wall for the Renault drivers. He says:

The Batak system allows the Renault F1 Human Performance Centre to accurately assess a driver's agility and motor response time to a set of random lights. This can be performed under normal or fatigued conditions to simulate the affect of a long race. The system incorporates elements of decision-making into some of the tasks to add a cognitive element to the tests. Tests can last anywhere from 30 seconds to 10 minutes – which can be extremely taxing.

Developing and improving your speed

Just like strength, speed is specific to the sport you compete in. You will find that top drivers are very quick with their hands and feet because they need the quick gear changes and fancy footwork in the car during the race.

It's true that some people are naturally faster than others. This, to some extent, results from their inherited muscle type. Broadly speaking there are three types of muscle fibre – Types I, IIa and IIb.

Type I fibres, also known as *red* or *slow-twitch* fibres, allow us to perform low-intensity exercises for longer periods, i.e. they have a higher aerobic capacity and therefore fatigue less quickly.

Type IIa fibres perform both low and high intensity work in moderate amounts.

Type IIb fibres, also known as *white* or *fast-twitch* fibres, have the potential to work extremely fast. However, they fatigue more quickly.

Do not despair if you think you are lacking in fast-twitch muscles. The good news is that research has shown that training improves both types, possibly fast-twitch muscles more than slow-twitch.

Speed training is best developed by simulating conditions that you will eventually be competing in. Try to replicate the motions that you expect to make during cornering, braking and so on, and add resistance to the movements. This method of training is well established with top athletes. For example, some sprinters sprint while towing a weight, such as a car tyre, behind them to create a resistance. Generally you will build up speed if you make your muscles contract rapidly against a low resistance. Try the following exercises designed to develop faster hands and feet for motorsport.

Faster hands

Boxers need fast hands for their sport. A boxing bag is therefore a good and inexpensive way of developing your hand speed. Strike the bag using fast and firm hits. Start off slowly and build up, at the same time keeping your strikes even. See how fast you can go without compromising on the quality of your strikes.

Another excellent way to test your reaction time and hand speed, as well as hand-eye co-ordination, is a currently available children's toy that involves hitting with a plastic mallet a target that pops up randomly. If played against an opponent it will give you an idea of how you stand. The same can be said for some arcade games. To get even closer to home, some drivers regularly play driving games such as *Colin McRae Rally* on their computers.

Racquet sports, such as squash, table tennis and badminton are excellent ways to hone your reaction time and hand-eye co-ordination. Carlos Sainz, twice FIA World Rally Champion was also Spanish junior squash champion. Jim Moodie and Alister McRae are regular squash partners whenever their busy racing calendars allow it.

Faster feet

A basic exercise is to start jogging on the spot and gradually build up the pace whilst remaining on the same spot. As your speed increases concentrate on taking controlled steps. They will naturally involve less knee lift and you may even find it easier to stoop slightly forwards as the speed increases.

Another simple drill, used regularly by the armed forces, involves the use of tyres laid flat. The idea is to make your way as fast as possible across the tyres by placing a foot in each tyre. Instead of tyres you can use markers such as items of clothing. For variety, do the exercises whilst facing sideways or even backwards.

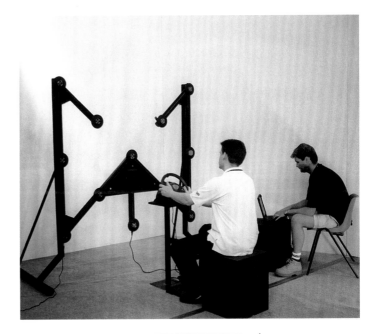

The Batak Wall, which measures your reaction time, co-ordination and balance, was invented by Dr David Nelson. It involves hitting the light as soon as you see it lit. The wall shown in the photograph is used by the Renault F1 drivers and was developed specifically for their purpose. Batak Walls are now commonly used in many sports disciplines. Further information may be obtained on www.batakpro.com. (Quotronics System Engineering)

Developing faster hands with the aid of a boxing bag. A martial arts focus glove is an alternative if training with a partner. (Mike Gibbon, MVG Photographic)

7 Spirit

Kimi Raikkonen at the wheel of his Sauber at the start of a Formula 1 Grand Prix. With just minutes to go before the start, this would be a useful time to visualise how the first corner may be taken.
(Red Bull/Sutton Motorsport)

There is undoubtedly a connection between the state of mind and performance of a competitor. This is being more widely recognised, and most top motorsport teams now have sports psychologists who use mental training to help their drivers to achieve peak performance. Most top motorsport drivers now have very similar skills, fitness levels and competition cars. This means the margin for success is often very slim and not uncommonly down to the competitor who remains focused.

The aim of this is to help you develop a state of mind which makes everything go your way on the day of the event. Some call it *being in the groove* or *being in the zone* or *on a roll*. Whatever it may be called, it is a great feeling of confidence that results in consistent results that may even supersede expectations.

How do you know when you have reached that state of mind? You will be mentally *aroused* but just about at the right level. You are *relaxed* so that your muscles are not tensed up. Your *confidence* in your own ability and that of your car or kart is such that you *expect* a reasonable result regardless of what may come your way. You are totally *focused* on the task in hand and do not allow any distractions to deter you from achieving your goal. You are getting immense *enjoyment* from the race, which seems to be progressing with minimum *effort* and almost *in slow motion* with you fully in *control*. Your racing lines are *smooth* and controlled. You hardly notice the spectators as you are *in charge*!

This is how champion rally-driver Louise Aitken-Walker felt when she was on a roll:

> When I was going well, I was going well! I was on a song and dance. And nobody could touch us. Nobody could beat us. To

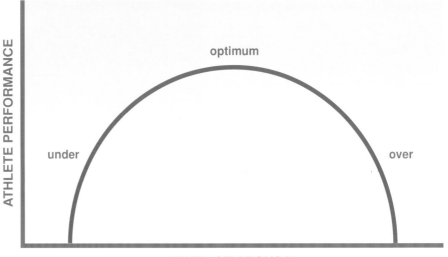

The inverted U shape that shows that optimum arousal is achieved by being neither over- nor under-aroused, but in the middle.

ATHLETE PERFORMANCE

optimum

under

over

LEVEL OF AROUSAL

have that feeling was fantastic. It was just exhilarating to drive as well as we did. We made history and it was great. You believe in yourself and think you can do the same again.

She described how over-arousal can occasionally lead to problems:

Then we had one of our biggest accidents ever in Kielder (Forest). Totally wrote off the car because we overdid it while on the song and dance.

Your arousal level

For peak performance you need to be at your optimum level of arousal. Too low or too high a level will be a hindrance, so it is important that you know how to hit your personal arousal level. There are several techniques for doing this and those commonly used in motorsport are:

- Relaxation
- Imagery
- Focusing
- Centering
- Positive self-talk
- Target-setting.

Relaxation
This is the key to success. You cannot have an anxious mind in a relaxed body or the other way round. Several relaxation techniques are available and, as with many things, what is successful for some may not work for others. Try them and stick with one that works for you, but do follow the basic guidelines given below when using your chosen technique. Commonly used techniques include the use of saunas, Jacuzzis, hot baths, massage and music. Massage in particular is useful for physically relaxing tense muscles, and can be used in conjunction with progressive muscle relaxation.

Before you start
- Practice makes perfect. The more you try the technique the more useful it will be.

- Avoid close-fitting clothing and noisy uncomfortable places when practising.
- Lie down if you have to but avoid falling asleep.
- Enjoy the sessions rather than force yourself to relax.
- Try to empty your mind when relaxing.

Progressive muscle relaxation
There are also many techniques for muscle relaxation. A commonly used one which has proved effective is progressive muscle relaxation. It involves tensing and relaxing muscle groups in sequence. Some start with their toes and move slowly towards their head. Other athletes choose only to relax the muscles they use in competition. For motorsport this is likely to be the upper body with specific attention to the arms, shoulders and neck. By tensing and relaxing each muscle group competitors will learn to appreciate signals from their bodies. This type of relaxation can be self-taught, or you can follow instructions on one of the commercially available audiocassettes.

Here is a suggested routine:

- Start with five to eight deep breaths while shrugging your shoulders and rolling your head slightly to relax your muscles.
- Then, once you are ready, inhale deeply using your abdominal muscles and tighten your feet muscles as much as possible and hold for a count of three.
- Relax your muscles as you exhale and imagine the stress leaving the relaxed muscles.
- Move higher up your body to the calf muscles and repeat the procedure. From there go on to the thighs (front and back), buttocks, abdominal muscles, lower back, chest, upper back, shoulders, biceps, triceps, forearms, hands, neck and face muscles.
- As you get better, you can reduce the time to total relaxation and even involve fingers, toes and other smaller muscles.
- About 20 minutes is a reasonable time to perform total body relaxation for the first time.

Imagery

Also known as visualisation, this is an extremely useful technique used by competitors in all sports. It involves visualising or seeing yourself in the race vehicle driving a particular circuit or stage. It's possible that you have already been practising a kind of imagery without being fully aware of it. For instance, when you have an important telephone call to make it is quite likely that beforehand you will practise in your mind what you want to say to give yourself a better chance of ensuring a successful outcome when you actually make the call. It is, effectively, psyching yourself up for the event ahead.

With practice you should be able to develop an emotional state close to what you expect to experience during the race. You will hear the engine revving, feel the force of the acceleration and the change in body position as you drive or power around corners. For some it can be helpful during visualisation to more closely simulate the real thing by adopting the driving position with hands on an imaginary steering wheel and feet on imaginary pedals.

The Italian Jordan Formula 1 driver Giancarlo Fisichella uses imagery as part of his preparation before races. He is able to visualise himself through the entire Monaco circuit with his eyes closed. In doing so he runs through all the gear changes, braking and acceleration strategies he expects to make in the actual race. Amazingly, the timing during these imagery sessions is usually within a few seconds of the practice laps.

Some athletes are known to practise visualisation regularly for 10 minutes every week, and as race day draws close they step this up to every day. However, because successful visualisation can arouse emotions as powerful as on the race day itself, it is generally not recommended that you practise it before bedtime!

You may find music an excellent motivator and trigger for imagery, but the type of music is important as loud aggressive music can elicit an inappropriately high arousal level.

Imagery is also helpful just before a race to get you into a *racing mind*.

Focusing

Sometimes described as being *on auto-pilot* or *being connected* or *with tunnel vision*, focusing is central to competition psychology. It means being relaxed and completely absorbed in your performance. From a safety point of view you are aware of everyone and everything around you, but you don't let the presence of anyone or anything interfere with your concentration.

There are many distractions in motorsport, such as worries about other drivers, the set-up of your car, a bad starting position, stalling on the grid, crashing out, your sponsors' expectations, your personal expectations and uncertain weather conditions. All these threaten to unnerve you, and the competitors who do best are those who can blot out these distractions and focus on the job in hand.

Like relaxation, focusing comes with practice. The better you get at it the easier it will be to recover from distractions such as spins on the track or road. There are several strategies to help you focus in sport. Not all of them work for everyone, so choose one that suits you and stick with it. Here are some tips to help you focus next time you compete or practise.

- Set out a mental game plan before each event or practice session. When your mind begins to wander, use the plan as a mental cue to help regain focus.
- Be realistic about your targets – your subconscious likes to know that your goals are achievable.
- Your focus will be better if you are physically ready for the race, so practice is important!
- Restore your focus by thinking positively after a setback. For example, following a distracting incident such as a wheel change mid-stage in a rally,

The Portugal Rally is infamous for its crowds. Knowing how to deal with distractions such as large crowds as seen here is important for any motorsport competitor. (Maurice Selden, Martin Holmes Rallying)

When relaxation means celebrating your birthday with loved ones, as Jensen Button looks set to do. (Sporting Pictures UK)

reassure yourself that you *can* complete the rest of the stage in your allotted time, and go for it!

- You obviously enjoy motorsport, and focusing comes much easier when you are enjoying what you are doing. Your enjoyment and focus will be enhanced when you are mentally and physically in peak condition.
- If your focus is starting to drift, remember your previous best performance. This will remind you of your feeling of success and will stimulate your mind to regain its focus and strive for that feeling again.
- Use visual cues in the car. I know a

driver who has a small card with *You're The Best!* written on it and taped to the sun visor of his race car. Although he knows he is not the best, he uses it as a cue to help him focus while racing. He has in fact finished most races he has entered.

Centering

This is a useful technique to either achieve or regain an optimum arousal level during a race or rally. It takes a few seconds once mastered and relies totally on breathing technique. It is easy to do and is extremely effective after a spin or a crash, for example, where controlling anxiety is

crucial. It needs practice, however, to master the technique.

- Make sure you are in quiet and comfortable surroundings and sitting when practising.
- Shrug your shoulders and roll your neck to relax your muscles.
- Start taking a long and deep breath in through your nose using only your abdominal muscles to draw the air in. Try not to use your chest muscles. If your technique is correct, your chest wall will not move as you breathe in.
- Focus at all times on your breathing and on using your abdominal muscles.
- Hold the inhaled breath for a count of two and then slowly exhale for a count of four.
- Do not use any muscles when breathing out – just allow your muscles to relax.
- As you breathe out you will experience a release of tension.
- Repeat the process five to eight times.

Centering should be practised until refocusing is possible with only a single breath and under race conditions. Do make sure, however, when you inhale and exhale that your mind is clear of all distractions.

Positive self-talk
This is a useful tool for regaining the appropriate arousal level. Its purpose is to flush from your mind all negative thoughts, such as '*I will never finish the stage on time*' or '*I will never overtake the car ahead!*' By using positive self-talk – literally giving yourself a pep talk – you can overcome defeatist feelings and set yourself up to fight back after setbacks.

Target-setting
The value of target-setting is not confined to sport; it's an essential exercise if anything really worthwhile is to be achieved in life. Positive self-talk can also be brought into play by articulating your preset targets during training or practising; for instance: '*I will complete the race circuit in less than three minutes by the end of the afternoon!*' Target-setting based on pre-event recce can prove particularly useful in stage rallying. Achieving your stage target times will stimulate your arousal level and will set you up for the following stages.

Some of the techniques described in this chapter can also be used during your usual training sessions at the gym. For example, having watched a Formula 1 race on television, our man Jim, the amateur rally driver, had a brief *imaging* session. He realises that he needs to reduce weight for the following season if his performance is to improve so he sets himself a target weight loss of 1 stone (6kg) over the next three months (*target setting*) which he achieves with some *positive self-talk* over the period.

Richard Burns, 2001 World Rally Champion, can be seen mentally pumping himself at the start of a stage. Imagery, positive self-talk, focusing and target-setting are all established routines in constant use by all top drivers. (Mike Gibbon, MVG Photographic)

8 **Balance,** agility and co-ordination

Evidence suggests that these aspects of fitness will be invariably developed as you train using the recommendations outlined in the previous chapters. They do, however, deserve special mention as they constitute important qualities that any motorsport competitor must have to be successful. Again, as with strength and skill, these qualities are sport-specific so by simulating the conditions likely to be encountered in motorsport they can be improved.

Balance, very simply, is the ability to keep the body in equilibrium. True enough, some individuals are better at it than others but the good news is that it can be improved with training and practice.

Agility is a component that top footballers and racquet players possess and constantly work on to improve. It is how fast the body can change direction and position. Obviously, it must do this gracefully and with balance or the quality becomes useless.

Co-ordination refers to the smooth execution of the specific task in hand. There is no doubt that this component comes with skill and technique. The more skilful a driver you are the better co-ordinated your movements. You apply the power at the right times in the corner; you correct under or over steer in fluid motions instead of jerky movements that fishtail the car all over the road. Like balance, co-

ordination comes with hours of practice. You must expose your body to the same task over and over again so the next time it is encountered, the body reacts to it on time, harmoniously and with poise.

Balance and co-ordination are more important than agility in motorsport. They come with practice and skill and as it is not the aim of this book to advise the reader on how to drive the race car, they are best learnt and developed in the race car. However, they are also a by-product of training in general and if you have been following the recommendations in the earlier chapters you will be working on your balance, agility and co-ordination.

The 1995 FIA World Rally Champion Colin McRae knows the importance of balance and co-ordination. He owns and flies a helicopter which requires a high level of spatial awareness in all three dimensions. Like rallying at the highest level, flying mandates the rapid processing of information and acting on it using all four limbs. Colin also enjoys motorcycling both on and off road. Trail biking is how he first started and up to this day he still uses it to improve on his fitness and performance.

David Coulthard of the West McLaren Mercedes Formula 1 team plays basketball and rock climbs to develop his balance and awareness.

Kimi Raikkonen doing wheelies on his mountain bike, demonstrating the co-ordination and balance required of top drivers.
(Red Bull/Sutton Motor Sport)

David Coulthard of McLaren-Mercedes F1 rock climbing. This improves balance and co-ordination, upper body muscles and spatial awareness. (Mike Gibbon, MVG Photographic)

Opposite: *Renault driver Jarno Trulli making his own strenuous ascent.* (Renault F1)

Squash is an excellent game for developing balance and co-ordination. Carlos Sainz, former FIA World Rally Champion and Ford Martini World Rally driver was also a national squash champion in Spain. Jim Moodie is seen playing here. He regularly challenges Alister McRae between races. (Mike Gibbon, MVG Photographic)

⑨ **Weight loss**
in motorsport

Nick Heidfeld tucks into fruit salad for dessert. A good choice. (Sporting Pictures UK)

There is no doubt that a lighter driver and lighter car move faster! In motorsport, acceleration usually matters more than top speed, and a lighter car and driver will accelerate faster out of corners.

Competitors usually have no hesitation in spending vast amounts of money to shave those extra grams off their equipment. An FIA-approved Kevlar competition seat costs three times as much as a standard fibreglass seat yet only weighs about 2.5kg (6lb) lighter. This could be achieved much more cheaply by losing 3kg of fat four to five weeks before the race. What competitors must realise is one of the greatest weights in a race car is the driver.

Many competitors need to achieve their ideal body weight. A recent survey of rally drivers participating in a national event found that as many as half were overweight in relation to their height. In fact some even classified as obese!

Obesity is now a serious problem. The World Health Organisation recognises it as a disease process, and the shocking fact is that the death rate and health problems associated with obesity in the western world now equals that caused by under nutrition in the developing world.

Am I overweight?

Although looking in the mirror is a simple way of working out if you are overweight, it is subjective because it depends upon how you see yourself. Measuring Body Mass Index (BMI) is a better method. Although still not ideal, it gives a more accurate indication of how overweight you are. BMI is calculated by dividing your weight (in kg) by the square of your height (in metres).

Let us take Jim, our amateur rally driver, as an example. He is aged 35, is 1.68m tall (5ft 6in), weighs 85kg (14.2 stone) and has a BMI of 30.4.

$$\frac{weight\ (kg)}{height \times height\ (m)} = BMI$$

$$\frac{85}{1.68 \times 1.68} = 30.4$$

The ideal BMI range is 19–25. Over 25 is considered to be overweight and those with a BMI over 30 are classified as obese.

Use the BMI chart to see what class you fall into.

Although many health professionals use BMI to assess health risk, it does have limitations. It assumes excess weight is excess fat and is therefore not suitable for competitors with well-developed musculature.

Weight classification according to Body Mass Index.

BMI	Class
<20	Underweight
20–25	Normal weight
25–30	Overweight
30–40	Obese
>40	Morbidly obese

Is my excess weight fat?

Most people believe that extra weight is extra fat. This is not the case at all. Body weight consists of lean tissue and body fat. Lean tissue is made up of water, muscle, organs and blood, and fat simply consists of FAT! The proportion of fat is affected by an individual's level of fitness.

The inactive and overweight competitor who eats a high-fat diet is likely to have an extra weight value that is mainly made up of fat rather than lean tissue. On the other hand, an active competitor on a relatively balanced diet who is overweight is likely to have more lean tissue than fat to account for the extra weight. If you really want to know how much fat you are carrying, then body composition measurements are necessary.

Many health and fitness clubs will measure body composition using skin fold callipers or bio-electrical impedance analysis (BIA). The callipers measure fat just underneath the skin at various places on the body, such as the hip area, the biceps, triceps and shoulder blade, among others. Using these measurements and other calculations, body fat percentages can be calculated.

BIA uses a small electric current that passes through the body. The fat cells act as a resistance to the current, while lean tissue is a good conductor of the current. The amount of resistance gives an indication of percentage of body fat. Make sure you are well hydrated when having a BIA measurement otherwise you will read a higher percentage body fat. There is no ideal body fat percentage. Different sports require different percentages, but in motorsport it is probably important that you stay as low as possible without compromising on other components of fitness. As a general guide, the percentage associated with the lowest health risk is 13–18% in males and 18–25% in females.

There are more accurate means for calculating body fat but these are rarely found outside research centres and hospitals.

So I'm overweight – how do I lose it?

There is no simple solution and what works for one person may be a complete disaster for another. Success rates often run low and when people get discouraged they fall back into their bad habits. The consolation is that the principles for losing weight are really simple and can be applied easily.

There are literally hundreds of health and fitness plans available from self-professed experts on weight loss, many of which are based on poor scientific principles. And the introduction of the Internet into everyday lives has done little more than to increase the confusion that already exists.

very obese

obese

overweight

healthy

underweight

A Body Mass Index chart extracted from the 'Body Mass Index Ready Reckoner' published by Servier Laboratories Ltd. Find your height in metres or feet and inches and your weight in kilograms or stones. The two readings meet at your BMI. (Courtesy: Servier Laboratories Limited 1997)

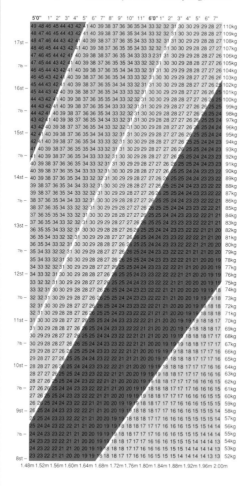

Put very simply, for weight loss to occur, energy expenditure (energy used by the body) must be greater than energy intake (food and drink consumed). This must be for a reasonably prolonged period of time and must result in the creation of an energy deficit.

One sure way of creating an energy deficit is to reduce or modify input. To better understand this it is important to have a working knowledge of Resting Metabolic Rate (RMR). This is the number of calories the body *must* have per day to keep essential body functions ticking over. RMR varies according to age and sex. To calculate your RMR use the table in *Fig. 1*.

RMR calculates the number of calories required assuming you are lying in bed for 24 hours doing nothing. Most people do not do that so the actual number of calories required per day varies according to their lifestyle. Those who are very active (labourers) generally need twice the RMR. To calculate your daily energy expenditure use the table in *Fig 2*.

Jim weighs 85kg and wants to lose weight for the following season. He is a garage owner who runs the business largely from behind a desk. He does, however, make regular visits to the working area during the day. From the table in *Fig. 51* his RMR is (85 x 11.6) + 879 = 1,865 calories (kcal). Given his lifestyle his daily expenditure is 1865 x 1.7 = 3,170kcal. To lose weight he must consume food and fluid that has a total calorie count of less than 3,170kcal in 24 hours.

Drastically reducing the calorie intake is not good for the body and does not shed fat any faster. The body will recognise such a drop in calorie intake as a sign of starvation and will begin to break down lean tissue instead of fat. The ideal method is to cut the daily calorie count by 15% and no more.

So, Jim needs to consume 85% x 3,170 = 2,695kcal every day for fat loss to occur.

Reducing calorie intake is only part of the game. The diet must also be modified to give a healthy balance of carbohydrate,

RESTING METABOLIC RATE CALCULATOR		
Age (years)	Male	Female
10–17	(wt in kg x 17.5) + 651	(wt in kg x 12.2) + 746
18–29	(wt in kg x 15.3) + 679	(wt in kg x 14.7) + 496
30–59	(wt in kg x 11.6) + 879	(wt in kg x 8.7) + 829

DAILY ENERGY EXPENDITURE	
Level of daily activity	Daily expenditure
Light (e.g. office job)	RMR x 1.55
Moderate (e.g. regular walking during day)	RMR x 1.7
Heavy (e.g. labouring)	RMR x 2.0

fat, protein and other essential components.

What's given here is a general guide only. More information on the subject can be obtained from books on nutrition or from recognised websites such as the Calorie Control Council. This organisation uses sound scientific research as a cornerstone to their published work which may be found on www.caloriecontrol.org.

What makes up a balanced diet?

A healthy balanced diet should have around 60% carbohydrate, 15% protein and 35% fat. Athletes change these figures to suit their individual sports. In motorsport generally, the leaner and lighter the competitor the better the outcome as long as you do not compromise muscle – so if you do choose a combination, go for one that aims for fat loss but preserves muscle.

Carbohydrates fuel all activities. Generally, the more you load up on carbohydrates the longer you can perform any activity. Carbohydrates are stored mainly in the liver and muscles. Top athletes tend to binge on high-carbohydrate

Fig. 1. Use this table to calculate what your daily Resting Metabolic Rate (RMR) should be in kcal. (Taken from 1985 FAO/WHO/UNO report)

Fig. 2. Daily Energy Expenditure is calculated by multiplying your RMR by a factor depending upon your level of activity during the day.

foods like pasta and potatoes before an event to give them more staying power. What motorsport drivers should eat, and what they should avoid, is covered later in this chapter.

Protein makes up most of your cell structures, including muscles, hair and nails. It is not a major energy source but is essential for repair. High protein intake has its value in pursuits such as weightlifting and bodybuilding, but for motorsport purposes there is little need to increase bulk, with its consequent weight gain, and a moderate protein intake is preferable.

Although fat is something that many people could do with shedding quite a bit of, it is nevertheless an essential component in our diets. Fat is important for insulation, long-term energy stores, hormones and the protection of organs. However, it's generally the amount and type of fat that you eat that could do with altering. Go for unsaturated fats and oils as they are less harmful to your body. Vegetable fats and oils are also generally better than animal fats.

If you are serious about eating a balanced diet, then try to keep a diet diary for a few days. You will probably be surprised how different your carbohydrate, protein, fat balance is from that recommended.

This is Jim's diet diary for a day

	kcal	carbo-hydrate	fat	protein
Breakfast				
1 bacon roll	275	52g	22g	8g
1 coffee	75	25g	2g	2g
(white, 2 sugars)				
Mid-morning				
Cola drink (reg)	145	37g	0g	0g
Cookies (2)	100	15g	3g	0.5g
Lunch				
Fast food burger	550	40g	33g	26g
French fries	320	16g	40g	4g
Milkshake	335	16g	8g	9g
Apple pie (1 slice)	345	51g	15g	3g
Mid-afternoon				
Iced bun	130	21g	5g	2g
1 coffee	75	25g	2g	2g
(white, 2 sugars)				
Dinner				
Chicken curry	800	80g	40g	100g
Naan bread (1)	420	66g	10g	2g
Onion Pakoras (2)	150	22g	6g	5g
Bottled beer	150	15g	0g	3g
TOTAL	3,870	481g	186g	166.5g

There are several problems with Jim's diet

1. Too many calories considering his lifestyle.
2. Too much fat. He is eating a lot of 'hidden fat' in the burgers, bacon roll and fries.
3. Too little fibre. 30g per day is recommended especially if trying to lose weight. High-fibre foods tend to be low in fat and also give the 'full belly' feeling.
4. Too little fluid. Coffee and alcohol dehydrate the body. Colas tend to have little or no nutrients.
5. Poor timing of meals. A high RMR is best maintained by eating regularly during the day instead of eating heavily at night as Jim does.

Eating a healthy and balanced diet is *not* that difficult and requires a bit of self-discipline to begin with. Once the pounds start to fall off, most people enjoy the lifestyle change, especially if their race and rally performances improve.

Jim decides to make a minor adjustment to his daily intake. He stops putting butter on

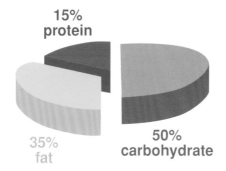

15% protein

35% fat

50% carbohydrate

A balanced diet.

his roll in the morning. Not too much of a sacrifice! This will save him about 40kcal per day, which translates to about 15,000kcal a year, or the equivalent of 2kg of fat!

The table in *Fig. 3* shows the calorie and fat content of commonly eaten food. Calories can be saved by switching to low-fat foods without 'dieting' or losing much in the way of taste.

Special diets

Some diets, like liquid diets (Slimfast) and the Aitken's Diet Plan are specialised. Their success rates are variable and the plans do not suit everyone. The Aitken's diet, for example, recommends a high-protein and low-carbohydrate intake. Although weight loss may occur, it may be at the expense of muscle mass rather than fat. Before starting specialised diets seek advice from a doctor or nutrition specialist, as certain medical conditions can be worsened.

The output

Remember from the energy balance equation that reducing the input is only half of the game. To create a negative balance, energy expenditure must also be increased and this is achieved by simply doing more exercise.

Physical activity accounts for around 25% of total daily expenditure in someone like Jim, while top athletes may expend up to 80%. This wide variation means that increasing exercise is a sure way of slimming down and shedding those surplus pounds of fat.

Apart from the obvious benefits of becoming fitter, increasing physical activity pays other dividends that include:

- Less likelihood of diabetes.
- Better body functions, such as lung capacity, endurance, joint functions, etc.
- Better balance of fats in the blood (some fats are better than others).
- Better blood pressure control.
- Less chance of mild clinical depression and anxiety (both more common in obese people).

Type	kcal	Fat	Substitute	kcal	Fat
Whole milk (1 cup)	170	8g	Semi-skimmed milk	120	3.0g
White bread (1 slice)	85	1g	Wholemeal bread	65	0.5g
Muffin (1 portion)	160	10g	Plain biscuits (2)	65	3.0g
Fries (1 portion)	320	40g	Baked potato	175	0.5g
Full fat cheese (1 slice)	100	9g	No fat cheese spread	25	0g
Butter	100	10g	Low fat spread	50	5.0g

- Improved self-esteem and general well-being.

As well as being overweight, bordering on obese with a BMI of 30, Jim has a family history of heart disease. His father had a heart attack at an early age. Jim can reduce his risk by losing weight and exercising more. Unfortunately, instead of using exercise to relax, he tends to do little over weekends. This creates a reduction in energy expenditure of about 500kcal a day at weekends, which multiplied by 52 weekends in the year, results in an overall positive balance of 52,000kcal a year, or 3kg of weight gain. Over 10 years he would put on 30kg, or 5 stone, in weight!

So what exercise should I do to lose weight?

As with any exercise plan it is recommended that you consult a doctor before starting, especially if you have not exercised for some time.

This chapter is not only for those who are overweight. It should also be useful as a general guide for those who want to maintain their weight during the race season.

The recommendations of the UK Health Education Authority in 1998 were: 'For improved health and to help in weight management, adults should try to build up gradually to take half-an-hour of moderate intensity physical activity on five or more days of the week. Activities like brisk walking, cycling, swimming, dancing and gardening are good options!'

Fig. 3. The change in kcal and fat by switching to other commonly eaten foods.

Stick to the following recommendations and you should lose weight:

- Exercise intensity should be to a level where you can just about talk without getting out of breath. Your breathing, however, should be slightly harder than normal.
- Go for 30 minutes of activity every day, even if it means three 10-minute periods or two 15-minute periods accumulated throughout the day.
- Consider going for longer sessions of up to 45 minutes to really shed the fat. This extended period of exercise uses fat as a preferential energy source and is also known as the 'slow-burn' by some.
- If you have a heart rate monitor, go for an intensity that keeps your heart rate at about 60% of maximum. If you are generally unfit you will be surprised at how low an intensity exercise is needed to reach this!
- Go for exercises that use the large muscles of the body and are aerobic (get you breathing hard and increase your heart rate). These include cycling, running and swimming.

Jim decides to make lifestyle changes. He continues to eat the same but increases his output by walking to work every day. This takes 20 minutes each way and at a leisurely pace burns 180kcal a day in total. At the weekends he decides to take up swimming for 30 minutes each day. Over three months he will burn 14,400kcal, or the equivalent of 1.6kg (3.5lb) of fat. All this without even modifying his input!

The table in *Fig. 4* shows the calories spent doing common activities over one hour for an average 70kg (11 stone) man. Remember that if you are heavier you will burn more calories.

How much should I aim to lose?

For best results weight loss should be gradual rather than sudden. That way, instead of fighting it, the body gets a chance to adjust to the loss.

Assuming you adjust your input and increase your output accordingly, and stick to this change, you can lose up to 2kg (4–5lb) in the first week. This is because most of the initial loss is owing to glycogen (a form of carbohydrate) breaking down and this requires a lot of water. Weight loss will slow down after this as fat begins to break down. This is not an indication that your plans have failed, so do not give up! If you lose around 0.5–1kg per week after the initial drop you will be doing well!

Some secrets of successful weight loss

The following tips are useful for competitors trying to balance their input and output.

- Avoid processed foods and meat products such as salami, beefburgers and sausages that have a lot of 'hidden' fat.
- Eat more fish, especially white fish that has very low fat content.
- Go for skimmed or semi-skimmed milk rather than whole milk. You will hardly notice the difference.
- Low-fat spreads have half the calories of margarine or butter and the taste is not too dissimilar.
- Beer and spirits have a huge amount of calories, so go easy if you can.

Fig. 4. The calories burnt doing everyday work. (Taken with permission from Calorie Control Council, www. caloriecontrol.org).

Activity	kcal per hour	Activity	kcal per hour
Aerobics	420	Soccer	480
Brisk walking	305	Stair climbing	630
Brushing teeth	175	Swimming	620
Gardening	335	Strolling leisurely	220
Jogging	695	Washing the car	315
Mowing the lawn	335	Watching TV	75
Playing cards	120	Weight lifting	215
Shovelling snow	415	Working at the gym	400

- Do not starve yourself as invariably you will more than make up for it at the next meal!
- Treat yourself occasionally as this takes away the urge to binge on the high calorie food.
- Set yourself a target weight in a reasonable target time instead of 'just losing some weight'.
- Encourage a partner to join you. This has been shown to have a higher success rate.
- Spread meals over the day rather than binge eat.
- Take on an activity that you enjoy instead of dragging yourself to the one that you don't.
- Weigh yourself regularly – it gives you encouragement to keep going.
- Don't fall into the self-pity trap. Everyone works as hard as you do and some even harder. You can always make time when you really want to!

What top drivers do

Colin McRae on his intake:

> I watch what I eat the whole time, especially the week before an event and during the rally itself. Eat lots of different things and the right amount of everything with not too much fatty and sweet stuff. Chicken, pasta, meat, fish and salads – basically a good Mediterranean diet …

and on his output:

> I cycle, do moto-cross, jet and water skiing … stuff that I enjoy doing otherwise it gets boring if you just jog around the block every morning.

Iain McPherson combines a variety of sport to keep his interest and fitness levels. He plays five-a-side football, uses mountain bikes, runs and plays badminton. During winter months he uses the gym.

Eating a balanced, healthy diet should not be that difficult.
(Sporting Pictures UK)

10 **Motorsport-** specific circuit training

This chapter brings together all the components of fitness into a motorsport-specific training circuit that can be done by all competitors regardless of their fitness levels.

Circuit training is a well-established and widely used method of training. It involves placing various exercises in a circular fashion using either the body weight as a resistance or equipment such as skipping

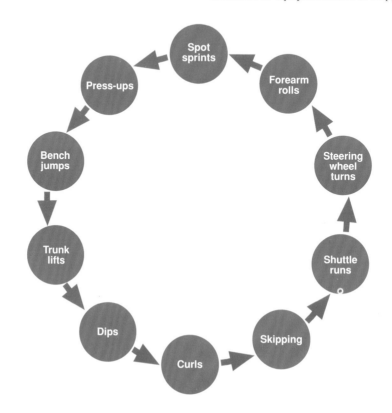

Organisation of a motorsport-specific circuit.

ropes, dumb-bells, etc. The circuit can be set either outdoors or indoors, for example in a gym. You then progress from one exercise to another and aim to complete the circuit in a set time. Each exercise in the circuit is designed to work a specific aspect of fitness.

There can be any number of exercises in a circuit but their sequence should be carefully organised so you do not stress the same part of your body at consecutive stations. Otherwise you will end up overworking the muscles involved. Although you want to prevent overload, it is important that at the end of each station you feel worked and close to tiring. As your fitness level rises you can challenge yourself by either reducing the rest period between a circuit or station, or simply increase the number of times you do the circuit.

Designing a motorsport-specific circuit

Motorsport-specific circuit training should include exercises that work the upper body, test aerobic endurance, help with balance and co-ordination and develop speed of movement in the limbs. The exercises should also burn sufficient calories to help combat excessive weight, and they can be combined with a reduction in the total calories ingested. The circuit as a whole should be mentally relaxing.

The circuit that follows is designed to achieve the above objectives. Start at any station but progress in order thereafter. Give yourself 30 seconds at each station in the first instance, followed by 30 seconds rest while you make your way to the next station. Do as many repetitions as possible during the workout time. As your fitness increases, aim for 60-second workouts and reduce the rest period. Always remember to warm up adequately before starting the exercises.

Station 1 – Press ups
Make sure that you keep your hands shoulder-width apart and your body rigid. If your fitness level is initially low, you may find it easier to do the exercise on your knees keeping your feet off the ground. See Chapter 4 on strength training for detailed advice.

Station 2 – Bench jumps
This exercise requires a low and stable bench about 12 inches off the ground. Stand astride it and jump up so that you land on it squarely and with your legs straight. Performed rapidly, the exercise works on balance, speed and co-ordination as well as lower body strength.

Station 3 – Trunk lifts
This workout is illustrated in Chapter 4 under back work. Trunk lifts are invaluable for lower back strength and spine stability.

Station 4 – Dips
Using a bench similar to that for Station 2, perform dips to work on the triceps, pectorals and latissimus muscles.

Station 5 – Abdominal curls
This workout is described in detail in Chapter 4. It exercises your abdominal muscles. To stress the internal and external oblique muscles, twist your trunk every alternate curl so your elbow meets the opposite knee. This exercise also helps back stability.

Station 6 – Skipping
A great exercise for co-ordination, balance and working the upper body. That is why boxers do it routinely.

Station 7 – Shuttle runs
Sprint as fast as possible for the pre-determined time between two markers set about 20–30 feet apart. Touch the marker with your hand at the end of each shuttle.

Bench jumps. (Mike Gibbon, MVG Photographic)

Steering wheel turns seen performed here by Iain McPherson, World Super Sport competitor, with the aid of a weight. (Mike Gibbon, MVG Photographic)

Opposite: For some teams yomping down sand mountains is all part of the fitness programme. Varied terrains test different parts of the body. (Renault F1)

Iain McPherson on forearm rolls. (Mike Gibbon, MVG Photographic)

Station 8 – Steering wheel turns

Stand with your arms straight out in front of you with your hands fisted. Make small semicircles with your hands so that you alternate which hand lies above the other, and continue doing this for the time allocated to the exercise station. This works your deltoid muscles as well as mimics the action of steering. As you speed up the exercise you work the muscles harder. Alternately try holding on to lightweight dumb-bells as you do the exercise.

Station 9 – Forearm rolls

Attach a weight on a string or cord to a bar. Hold it out in front of you with your arms straight and roll it gradually so that the string or cord winds onto the bar. This is a good exercise for your forearm muscles.

Station 10 – Spot sprinting

Start by jogging on the spot. Build up your speed so you take smaller and more rapid steps on your toes and maintain the rhythm until the pre-determined time is over.

11 **The** event

This chapter gives you guidelines on what to do and what to avoid during the days leading up to an event. The advice is based on scientific and medical principles currently applied by many athletes, and there is no reason why these principles cannot be adopted by motorsport competitors to give them the racing edge on the day. There are many types of motorsport events ranging from short sprints, such as drag racing, to ultra-marathons, like the Paris-Dakar rally lasting over 20 days, but whilst competitor requirements will vary from event to event, the basic principles remain the same.

Training

In the week of the event training intensity should be reduced gradually, and only a light session consisting largely of warm-up routines is recommended on the day before the event. This may be an option for professional drivers with teams responsible for race preparation. With amateurs, however, the day before the race is usually hectic and stressful. Although you may not think so, a visit to the gym may just be the thing to relax. Do try to fit in a light session or a slow jog the day before the race if at all possible. It will probably do little for you physically but do not underestimate the psychology. Many drivers will spend 30 minutes stretching at the gym with background music, followed by a sauna to help with visualisation and relaxation.

Meals

Dietary manipulation is a recognised method of maximising performance; even the ancient Olympians recognised this. The general consensus is that you should try to load up on carbohydrates in the days before the event. This will increase the glycogen levels in your muscles. Glycogen is what the body prefers to use during exercise and it is the depletion of this important carbohydrate that causes fatigue. The capacity of muscle to store glycogen increases with training, so by loading up before the event you decrease the chances of fatigue during the race. Carbohydrate loading should ideally start in the week before the event. Examples of carbohydrate-rich food are rice, pasta, noodles and potatoes.

The 72 hours before an event are particularly important for maximising muscle levels of glycogen, so aim for up to 70–80% of total intake from your meals to be carbohydrates if you can. Increasing glycogen levels is of special fatigue prevention benefit with endurance races lasting typically more than 1–1½ hours, but even with shorter events stores must be maximised, especially if there is little chance of topping up levels during the day of the event. Beware, though, that glycogen loading may cause a weight gain of around 1kg (2½lb) as extra water is needed to store it.

Hydration

It is much easier to hydrate fully in the 72 hour run-up to the event than to leave it to the night before, and it would be a major mistake to start an event in a dehydrated state. If you were to do so you would risk heat exhaustion, especially in the close confines of a cockpit and wearing a three-layer fireproof suit. In the WRC Safari Rally cockpit temperatures may be as high as 55°C and if you start the race behind in fluid intake it is highly unlikely you will be

In 1982 the Medical Commission for FISA issued guidelines for fluid intake in Formula 1 racing. It was recommended that drivers should drink 5 litres on race day. Juan Pablo Montoya complies. (Sporting Pictures UK)

able to make up the deficit considering you may lose as much as a litre for every hour you sit in the car. With only around four service stops per leg, lasting around 20 minutes each, it means you have to drink almost constantly.

If you are dehydrated you will produce urine less frequently and in smaller quantities as the body conserves all the water it can. The colour of the urine also tends to be darker and it may have a strong smell to it. You should learn to recognise your hydration status from your urine colour and from what your body tells you, i.e. your symptoms. Use a urine colour chart to maintain a reasonable hydration level. The symptoms of early dehydration include fatigue and headache. Increase your fluid intake if these symptoms are present.

Assessing urine colour is a good method of evaluating hydration status and has been used by many national teams such as the England cricket squad during tours in hotter countries. Competitors should aim for pale straw-coloured urine. Reprinted, with permission, from L.E. Armstrong, 2000, 'Performing in extreme environments' (Champaign, IL: Human Kinetics)

What you drink will depend on what you do in the days leading up to the event. If you are training, then a sports drink with carbohydrate content may be needed to provide energy as well as fluid. Otherwise, plenty of water, flavoured or not, should be sufficient. Remember that drinking regular soft drinks will give you a large calorie boost that you may not need. They may also contain caffeine that will dehydrate you. Because of this it is advisable to avoid coffee and soft drinks in the 72 hours before the event. Remember, too, that alcohol is a potent dehydrator!

What top drivers do

Colin McRae:
I don't drink alcohol at all during the recce, and if I know that an event is going to be particularly tough I won't drink at all in the week before I leave. Can be particularly tough when all your mates are off down the pub and going out, but it's really important to keep hydrated and in training.

Iain McPherson:
During a race weekend it is important also to relax, either by watching a video or television in the motorhome, or by going to the swimming pool for a swim and a sauna and jacuzzi.

The night before the event

This is undoubtedly a crucial time for all competitors, but instead of paying attention to maximising performance potential for the event the next morning, most of them are more likely to be found in the bar, until quite late, catching up with old friends and competitors. It's something they'll probably regret in the cold light of day.

It is best to avoid alcohol altogether. Should you have a drink, try to drink water before going to bed. There is a clear relationship between human performance and hydration status. Dehydration of as little as 2% of body weight (1.4kg or

1,400ml in a 70kg competitor) will cause you to feel thirsty and uncomfortable, and it will reduce your performance in endurance events. Up to 4% water loss (2.8kg or 2,800ml in a 70kg competitor) will reduce performance, lower urine output and lead to early fatigue. You may also experience nausea and vomiting. A 5% loss has been shown to reduce aerobic capacity by 30%. A loss of up to 6% (4.2kg or 4,200ml in a 70kg competitor) will affect concentration. Losses beyond this are dangerous as they cause physical weakness and confusion.

In 1982 the Medical Commission for FISA issued guidelines for fluid intake in Formula 1 racing. This followed Nelson Piquet's podium collapse from dehydration after his win at the Brazilian Grand Prix the same year. It was recommended that drivers should drink 5 litres on race day.

Sleep

Top athletes routinely retire to bed early the night before an event. Not only do they

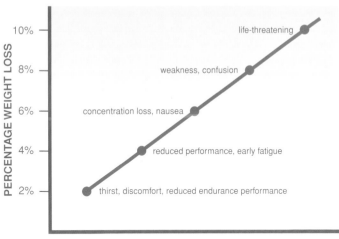

gain valuable rest, they also make time to prepare themselves mentally using techniques such as some of those described in Chapter 7. However, in amateur motorsport adequate sleep is sometimes difficult with the stress of the approaching event, especially for those competitors who also double up as the main organiser of their racing team. Don't underestimate the value of a good night's sleep, and try your level best to get at least 8–10 hours of quality shut eye.

The relationship between dehydration and human performance.

The podium collapse from dehydration. This incident, involving Nelson Piquet, led to the development of guidelines on fluid intake. (Mike Gibbon, MVG Photographic)

Some rounds of the World Rally Championship are notorious for their high temperatures. FIA-regulated three-layer fireproof race suits can act as a barrier to sweat loss that can exceed a litre for every hour in the car. The competitor seen here has lost so much sweat that the dye from his race suit has come off onto his T-shirt. (Maurice Selden, Martin Holmes Rallying)

Psychology

Many competitors find imagery (visualisation) particularly useful the night before the event, but don't do it just before trying to sleep as it can bring about emotions similar to those during the race. By this time most competitors will be familiar with the race circuit or have an idea of the stages involved and this, of course, helps the visualisation. The night before a race is also a good time to set some targets, taking into account the starting order and the opposition, and also to practise some positive self-talk. Any anxiety can be countered by progressive muscle relaxation.

What top drivers do

Louise Aitken-Walker:
I'd go to bed fairly early. I shut myself in my room and watch telly, read a book and completely chill out. I had to keep myself as calm as I could be.

Iain McPherson:
It is good to feel a bit of pressure before a race. It shows that you are switched on. You should be focusing only on the race, and entering the race confident that you've trained hard and that you are confident in your abilities. Nothing else should enter your mind. I sometimes tell myself that this will be the last day I live, so I can push myself to the limit.

Bernie Shrosbree:
This is what Bernie recommends for the competitors he looks after:

The night before a race it is a good idea to eat a light meal fairly early, maybe perform some light mobility work or easy cardiovascular training (e.g. a brisk walk) to aid relaxation and focus. If available, a massage can be of benefit, or a swim if facilities allow.

The morning of the event

This is probably the most anxious time for most! Each one has their own way of coping with pre-competition nerves and whatever works for you, stick with it!

Always rise early, at least three hours before the event starts. Getting dressed should be at a leisurely pace. Aim to be at the event venue at least 1 to 1½ hours before the start. En route to the venue use any aids that work for you. Some like to keep quiet and focused, while others recommend listening to music. Whatever your routine, try to keep it specific every time you race so it optimises your arousal. Specific routines have been shown to improve consistency of results.

Pre-event meal

Do not compete on an empty stomach, otherwise you risk fatigue and poor performance!

Try to eat a substantial meal at least 2–3 hours before start time. Delaying it will mean a full stomach at the start, and not only will this make you feel uncomfortable but vital blood flow that is more useful in the muscles will be diverted to the gut. Although some competitors may swear that eating certain foods on the morning of the event improves performance, there is little supporting evidence. But, if you find that something does seem to work for you, then continue to use it. The psychology is just as important as the physical benefit.

Most of the energy for the race will come from the food eaten in the days before the event rather than the pre-event meal. In endurance races, however, some energy may be drawn from the morning meal, so try to make it high in carbohydrate content. Several enjoyable foods can provide the necessary carbohydrates. These include breakfast cereals, muffins, crumpets, toast, potato cakes and waffles. If your anxiety level is running high, then eating may be the last thing on your agenda, but you must eat at least something, even if it is in fluid form – for example, a banana milkshake, custard, porridge or rice pudding.

Try to avoid fried or salted food. This usually leads to an uncomfortable sensation of thirst that may be troublesome on top of the dry mouth that usually comes from pre-competition nerves.

One word of warning! The morning of the event is not the time to experiment with new cereals or fibre foods. Do so at the risk of increased flatulence!

At the race venue

This is an important time for most as a good deal of mental preparation is done here. Again, stick with techniques that have worked for you in the past. Some competitors are remarkably quiet while others prefer company. Some have been known to suddenly become religious at this point! The key point is to get your body and mind ready to work at their optimum operating capacity.

Remember that in a very short time and during the race, your body will be physically subjected to jolts, bumps and g-forces – some very sudden and unexpected. Although the training in the days leading up to the event will have prepared you for this, it is important that you prevent injury and improve performance by getting your body into optimum shape just before the start. Boxers provide a good example of

The author stretching just before a stage of the Safari Rally, round of the World Rally Championship.
(Mike Gibbon, MVG Photographic)

Stretching of the levator scapulae that will be subjected to strong g-forces during cornering. (Mike Gibbon, MVG Photographic)

physical preparation before competition. As they enter the boxing arena they are usually coated with sweat having adequately prepared not too long before the fight. The blood flow to their muscles is optimal and they are ready for anything!

There are many techniques the motorsport competitor can use at this crucial time. Adequate warm-up and stretching of muscles and joints that will be in action is a recommended method. The advantages of a warm-up are several and were discussed in Chapter 2. A warm-up at this point will increase the blood flow, and therefore oxygen supply, to your muscles. They will then contract more efficiently and the chances of injury will be reduced. Just as important, a good warm-up will help with mental focus and relaxation.

An adequate warm-up at the event venue may be achieved more quickly with your race suit on as this will retain the heat generated. Recommended routines include jogging on the spot or brisk walking. Stretching of muscles specific to the sport

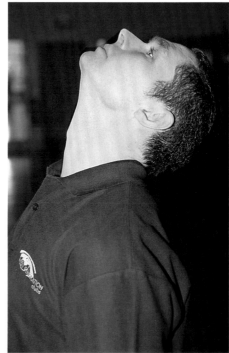

Flexion and extension of the neck through its full range. (Mike Gibbon, MVG Photographic)

and about to be used is another excellent technique. Lengthy routines may not be possible at race venues but it's advisable to do as much as you can as the advantages of doing a warm-up far outweigh the disadvantages. There may be an opportunity when changing into your race suit. Swimmers usually perform stretches at this point in the privacy of the changing room, so there's no reason why you cannot do so. Some stretches can even be performed in the race car while waiting for the start.

In temperate climates a total of about 15 minutes warm-up is probably sufficient before most motorsport events. If you have built up a light sweat then you have done well. Do make sure that your routine is not performed too early before the race, otherwise you will cool down. As a rule try not to warm up longer than 30 minutes before the start.

It is important to stretch the joints and muscles likely to be used in the event to their full range. In motorsport it is the

Shoulder rolling in both directions to prepare the deltoid muscles. (Mike Gibbon, MVG Photographic)

It is important that you get your body into optimum shape before the start of an event. (Sporting Pictures UK)

Stretching the triceps and shoulders. (Mike Gibbon, MVG Photographic)

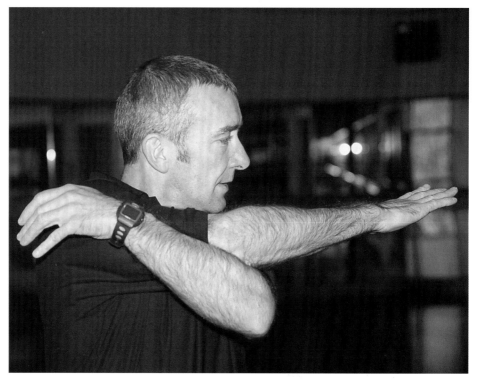

upper body, arms and neck which will take the brunt of the tremendous forces, and if the affected muscles and joints are not first moved throughout their full range prior to the race in a controlled and smooth fashion, it is highly likely that damage will occur when a jolt during the race *forces* them to their extreme, especially if the body is not warmed up. The motorsport-specific stretches recommended in Chapter 5 are ideal for this purpose. Remember, stretch slowly and gently but never till it causes pain.

Using a prop such as a wall to stretch the biceps and pectoral muscles in front of the chest. (Mike Gibbon, MVG Photographic)

Both the forearm muscles and the wrist joints are being worked on during this manoeuvre. (Mike Gibbon, MVG Photographic)

Mental preparation at the race venue

Remember that mental preparation comes with practice. If you have been practising regularly, the mental techniques described in Chapter 7 will come easier to you at this particularly anxious time. An especially useful method is imagery or visualisation. Downhill skiers are good examples of athletes who use imagery. Just before they begin their run down the mountain, as they wait for the start buzzer, competitors can be seen with head down and eyes closed visualising their descent right up to the finish line.

Centering is also a useful technique while at the start line, especially to relieve high anxiety levels. Although a harder method to master, with practice it can dramatically reduce anxiety with only a single breath.

Hydration

If you get to the race venue well beforehand, start your fluid intake so you drink about 500ml (½ litre) around two

A driver at a Formula 3000 race meeting. The driver is visualising on how to approach the first corner to gain advantage. At this point the competitor's attention is totally focused on the task in hand. (Red Bull/ Bernhard Spöttel)

hours before the start. This will allow any extra water to be lost as urine before the race. Then, just before the race, take in 125–250ml (1–2 small cupfuls). These are recommendations made by the American College of Sports Medicine. Try to drink as much as you comfortably can. Medical research has shown that large volumes of fluid in the stomach lead to faster emptying into the gut, which then leads to faster fluid replacement.

What top drivers do

Louise Aitken-Walker:

I just didn't go near people. I kept away from people because they can talk you into things. People can throw you off the line.

Bernie Shrosbree:

Early starts in rallying make extra demands on the driver and co-driver. It is important to get the body and mind ready for the race by performing some light exercise, eating a light breakfast, taking a shower and starting the hydration process for the day with sports drinks and water.

Iain McPherson:

His training intensity and quality three days before the race is restricted to a light run round the circuit. No exercise is taken the night before and on the morning of the race a light stretch is undertaken. As for the meal content, from three days before to the morning of the event the diet consists generally of pasta, bread and bananas, or foods of similar nature. He keeps himself hydrated at all times, taking energy drinks before and during practise runs. Iain tries to keep a constant sleep pattern over race weekends – in bed by 9.30pm and lights out by 10.00pm.

During the race

Even once the event has started there are ways, apart from your driving skills, to

make sure you retain the edge on the competition.

It is vital that you keep well hydrated during the race. Not only does the muscular effort of driving increase body temperature, the fireproof overalls, helmets, closed cockpits and heat radiation from the engine all make the situation worse than in most other sports. Research on Formula 1 drivers has shown sweat loss of up to 1 litre per hour while driving. In the Le Mans endurance race drivers have been recommended to drink as much as 1.3 litres for every hour they drive.

A good way of monitoring fluid replacement is by the colour of your urine (see urine chart at the beginning of this

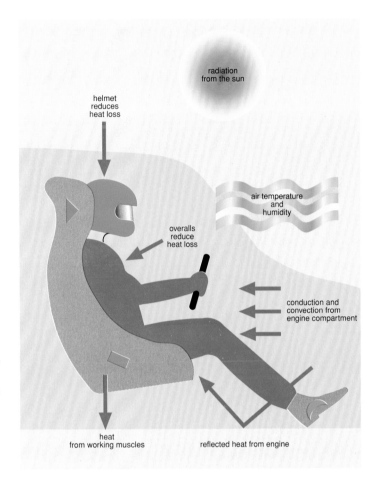

Heat production during motor racing. The competitor generates heat by muscular work. Conduction from the engine, the closed cockpit environment and race overalls all increase the body temperature and rate of sweating.

radiation from the sun

helmet reduces heat loss

air temperature and humidity

overalls reduce heat loss

conduction and convection from engine compartment

heat from working muscles

reflected heat from engine

François Delecour, former Ford WRC driver, drinks from a flexible hose attached to a commercially available drink bladder strapped to the back of his competition seat. The spring-loaded valve or bite-valve easily allows regular sipping of fluids during the event. A water bottle may also be attached to the roll cage within easy access of the driver. (Anwar Sidi, Sidi's)

than an hour, then use fluids with a carbohydrate content to provide energy. These have been shown to enhance performance. Commercially available sports drinks such as *Red Bull*, *Gatorade*, *Isostar* and *Lucozade* are examples of those that provide energy. Most sports drinks contain around 7% carbohydrate, so drinking 1 litre will provide around 200–300 calories.

Whilst water is the obvious choice if you want to simply hydrate yourself, medical research has shown that hypotonic drinks will do the job faster. Hypotonic drinks have a lower electrolyte (salt) concentration than the body and are therefore absorbed through the gut more quickly. Most commercial sports drinks are isotonic and have the same electrolyte concentration as the body. These are absorbed as fast as or faster than plain water. So, if rapid replacement of fluids to counter dehydration is a priority then go for hypotonic or even isotonic drinks rather than plain water. They will also probably be more palatable. Isotonic sports drinks are less dilute than hypotonic drinks because they contain carbohydrate for energy. They are therefore a compromise between energy provision and fluid replacement.

Each competitor will have his or her own drinking preferences during competition. You are the best judge of your own drinking pattern and style. I do suggest that you try all commercially available drinks and settle with one that you like, but the day of the event is not the time to experiment. Here are some useful tips:

chapter). This method is as good as laboratory methods for assessing hydration status. Aim for a pale straw coloured urine in copious quantities. Scanty volumes of dark urine suggest dehydration. Another method is by regular weighing while racing. Aim for a replacement of ¼ litre for every ½kg loss and you should be able to keep up with losses. Obviously, more fluid will be needed in hotter climates or if salty food is being eaten during the race. Remember that although thirst may drive the competitor to drink, it is not the best guide to replacing fluid loss.

Drinking during racing serves two main purposes – to prevent dehydration and to provide energy. The composition of the drink will depend on which of the two you are aiming for. If you are racing for more

- Hydration status is directly related to performance so do not ignore fluid replacement.
- Start off well hydrated. Ignore this at your peril! Once hydrated at the start you only need to top-up regularly as you lose fluids.
- Aim to maintain pale coloured urine in copious quantities.
- Aim to replace every 0.5kg weight loss during competition with at least ¼ litre

of fluid, i.e. always higher than what you have lost.

- Remember thirst is not the best indicator of your hydration status.
- If the race is longer than an hour, try to take in carbohydrate drinks to provide energy.
- If dehydration is a problem, choose isotonic or hypotonic drinks rather than plain water.
- Most commercial sports drinks are isotonic and are formulated to provide a balance between fluid replacement and energy provision.
- Fruit juices and fizzy drinks can initially dehydrate the body because of their high electrolyte (salt) content. They are therefore not ideal for rapid fluid replacement.
- If space and race format allows it, use a sports drink bladder with a flexible hose in your vehicle. Sports bottles are easy to use and have been shown to encourage drinking.
- Use cool water to make the drinks more palatable and help lower body temperature.
- Settle beforehand with a drink that you like. If none appeals to you then make your own sports drink as shown below.

The table gives recommendations for the type and routine of drinking during a race.

Outside temperature is also important when it comes to the type of drink consumed. In hot climates the competitor will sweat more and fluid replacement will be a priority over energy replacement. Hypotonic drinks will therefore have to be used. In the cold, isotonic drinks are more important.

Making your own hypotonic and isotonic drinks

Commercially available isotonic and hypotonic sports drinks can be expensive. You can easily make your own, and often they are more palatable. Try the following suggestion for home-made hypotonic and isotonic sports drinks.

Hypotonic drink – ideally for rapid fluid replacement

- Pure fruit juice 25% and plain water 75% with ¼ teaspoon salt per litre (optional).
- Fruit squash 10% and plain water 90% with ¼ teaspoon salt per litre (optional).

Isotonic drink – ideally for energy replacement

- Pure fruit juice 50% and plain water 50% with ¼ teaspoon salt per litre (optional).
- Fruit squash 20% and plain water 80% with ¼ teaspoon salt per litre (optional).

The optional addition of a small amount of salt is to provide the drinks with the necessary electrolyte balance and replace

Recommended drinking patterns and content for various motorsport races.

Type of Race	Suggested Drinking Routine & Drink
Regular heats lasting less than 30 minutes, e.g. karting events.	Hydrate fully before race. Replace losses with water or hypotonic fluid between heats. Weigh between races if possible and assess urine colour as day progresses.
Regular races lasting longer than 30 minutes.	Hydrate fully before race. Replace losses with hypotonic drinks. Weigh between races if possible and assess urine colour as day progresses.
Races longer than an hour with regular stops, e.g. stage rallies with road sections between stages.	Hydrate fully before race. Replace losses with hypotonic fluids stored in vehicle and replace energy with isotonic carbohydrate-based drinks at service breaks. Weighing and assessment of urine colour important.
Races lasting several hours with few breaks, e.g. endurance races, long-stage rallies.	Hydrate fully before race. Replace fluid and energy losses with hypotonic fluids and isotonic carbohydrate-based drinks stored in vehicle and at pit stops. Weighing and assessment of urine colour important at beginning and end of race to replenish total losses. If not possible, aim for 1300-1500ml for every hour in the car as an approximate guide.

losses through sweat. Pure fruit juice is typically hypertonic (more concentrated than body fluids) so it will tend to initially dehydrate you. Carbonated drinks provide about the same rate of fluid replacement as still drinks but are associated with a higher incidence of heartburn and a bloated feeling. Most drivers prefer still drinks, but if you opt for the carbonated kind then remember that 'diet' and 'low-calorie' drinks provide little or no energy. Their rate of fluid replacement is as fast as plain water.

What about caffeine?

Caffeine is actually a banned substance by the International Olympic Committee (IOC) Medical Commission. Although small amounts are acceptable, a urine concentration of greater than 12g/ml is considered to be a positive result. There is considerable individual variation when it comes to caffeine metabolism but as a rough guide a greater than 12g/ml urinary concentration may be achieved with about eight cups of coffee or 16 cans of cola over two to three hours. Competitors of small stature who are not used to consuming coffee regularly can have illegal urine levels of caffeine with less than eight cups.

There is no doubt that caffeine has its benefits and drawbacks when it comes to motorsport. On the positive side, most competitors and researchers will agree that it boosts concentration and mental alertness and improves reaction times. It also delays fatigue. For many it also provides a psychological prop. On the

down side, it can result in anxiety and irritability, which can compound the problem of pre-competition nerves. Taken at the wrong time caffeine can cause insomnia and deprive the competitor of much needed sleep. Possibly the most significant drawback of caffeine is its effect on dehydration. Not unusually used to kick-start the body and mind on the morning of the event by competitors who have possibly had too much alcohol the night before, it tends to further dehydrate and therefore impair driving performance.

Although widely used by motorsport competitors during an event for reasons outlined above, caffeine will not improve performance and you must be aware of its diuretic effects that can work against you if you do not keep up with the replacement of fluid losses. Like alcohol, caffeine is best avoided in the days leading up to an event.

Food

To maintain performance during competition you need the sort of solid food that will provide energy without dehydrating you excessively. The recommended and easy-to-eat foods include breakfast cereal or fruit bars, dried fruit, commercially available energy bars, bananas and sandwiches with fillings such as jam or honey. Most solid food requires additional water to digest and process it. Make sure you take in extra water.

Things to avoid are:

- Excessively spicy food, as this can cause unpleasant reflux and discomfort.
- Excessively salty food which may result in an unpleasant sensation of thirst.
- Unfamiliar food. The day of the event is not the time to experiment with food.
- High-fibre food, especially if your body is unaccustomed to it.
- Excessively fatty food.
- Low-carbohydrate food, as this depletes the body of much needed energy.
- Difficult to digest foods, such as steaks, that may give you a bloated feeling.

Some sports drinks, like Red Bull (45-kcal/100ml), designed to provide energy have been subjected to medical testing. This graph shows some results of a study done at University of the West of England. Researchers found that Red Bull boosted endurance significantly compared to a control drink. (Alford, C. et al. 'The Effects of Red Bull Energy Drink on Human Performance and Mood', Amino Acids 21, 2, 139-150, 2001)

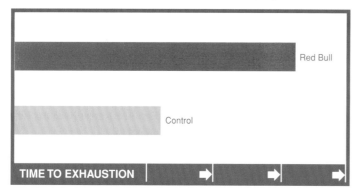

TIME TO EXHAUSTION

Red Bull

Control

The psychological perspective

Be at your best! Stay relaxed, be safe, keep focused on the event and let no-one and no thing distract you.

Those who have spun off during a race and have found themselves at the back of the pack will know the feelings of anger, self-directed disgust or depression that follow. Do not let such setbacks put you down and hinder your race progress. With a spin, use it as a reminder to take the same corner more skilfully next time you negotiate it. The best competitors always learn from their mistakes. If you made the error during practice you will have time to get it right in the race. If not, you can still learn as you compete. Combine the released energy from the anger you feel with some positive self-talk – *'be ready for it next time'* or *'this time get the car around faster'* – and you will notice the difference. You cannot be angry with yourself and at the same time give the race your best! You can, on the other hand, learn from the setback and get control of your emotions before they get control of you!

What separates the best from the rest is the ability to recover and readapt after stressful incidents. I still wonder how top Formula 1 drivers can walk away from dramatic crashes during practice and climb into the spare car within minutes to perform just as well and sometimes better. Or how top rally drivers calmly restart their mangled cars after overturning several times, and accelerate away seemingly oblivious to the incident.

Remember this golden rule and you will do well. *Potential distractions only become distractions if you let them distract you.* Take them in your stride as part of the race day and they will soon be forgotten. Dwell on them, or get stressed by them, and your performance will invariably suffer. Try the following tips to keep you in your stride next time you are faced with a potential distraction:

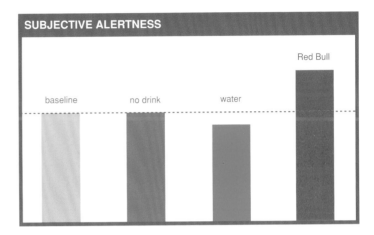

SUBJECTIVE ALERTNESS

baseline   no drink   water   Red Bull

- Decide on a game plan before the race and refer to the 'bigger picture' of success every time you feel distracted.
- Remember that on race day the crowds will be bigger, competitors (including you) will be more on edge. By retaining certain expectations you make the distractions less intrusive.
- *Expect the unexpected!* No competitor wants to crash during a race but the nature of the sport dictates that at some point in their careers most will. So when a crash does occur it is accepted as a risk of the sport and it fails to impact on competitor performance.
- *Knowledge is power!* Try to get as much information about where you are racing if you have not been there before. Ask other competitors or local clubs. Find out about the venue, the anticipated crowds, the accommodation and so on and you will not be surprised when you turn up on race day.
- Try your level best to keep positive about the distractions. Do not waste valuable time or effort on expressing anger or disappointment in them.
- Try to begin the race in a positive frame of mind. Any distractions will have less impact if you make a good start.

There is a driver who started competing at national stage rallies with a very low budget and his car was self-prepared,

Red Bull contains both caffeine and taurine for their beneficial effects. Both reaction times and alertness are increased if caffeine is taken in moderation. The graph here shows that Red Bull increased alertness in 14 subjects in comparison to their baseline, with no water or water alone. (Alford, C. et al, 'The Effects of Red Bull Energy Drink on Human Performance and Mood', Amino Acids 21, 2, 139-150, 2001)

under-powered in its class and was made up mostly of standard parts from the salvage yard. He was always up against better cars in his class but almost always finished events. He was also, by default, usually the top in his class. He admitted that his consistency was down to a mental game plan that he always stuck to. He would decide beforehand to run his own race and compete against no one but the clock. He was always fully aware but not flustered by the fact that others were in better cars. He knew that by trying to finish well in their class, other drivers would make mistakes. He capitalised on their errors and slowly improved his skills. Soon he was the one the crowd cheered, and in two seasons he had secured sponsorship to move on to a better car. He is a great example of someone who used positive thinking and adhered to a mental game plan to keep himself in control.

Should a distraction affect you then it is important your mind recovers fast. Many psychologists and team coaches purposely create distractions such as bad calls or large noisy crowds during training sessions to simulate what may happen during competition. Creating such distractions during motorsport can be dangerous, given the nature of the sport, so more often than not the competitor meets them for the first time on the day of the event. To learn to refocus, set some time aside beforehand to create such distractions in your mind and plan a response strategy. Settle on a plan that revolves around keeping positive, in control and calm. Use a physical or verbal cue to get you started. Even a *'come on, let's get on with the race'* may be the trigger you need either from yourself or your co-driver to refocus.

What top drivers do

Louise Aitken-Walker:
If anyone knows about keeping calm during accidents and recovering from them, then its Louise Aitken-Walker. Still talked about is her famous accident at the Rally of

Portugal in 1990, referred to earlier in the book, when her car slid off the road and rolled down a 150-foot cliff into a deep river. The car came to a stop upside down and fully submerged in 20 feet of water. In her own words:

> We were on slick tyres and the heavens opened. I can remember we were doing well. We were coming down this bit of road, came round the corner and the car just slid. I tried to turn the steering wheel but just swished off the edge. I knew there was going to be a big accident and just thought we have to get this over with. And, of course, we rolled and rolled and rolled down the mountain. The glass was flying around and suddenly we were submerged in water. We went right to the bottom and I thought, 'I can handle this!' It was pitch black and I was hanging upside down. I was totally calm, totally calm. I undid the seatbelt and slowly came out. I tried the windscreen first but got out of the door thinking, 'I am going to live!'

This is how she regained her composure after less dramatic crashes.

> The first time I crashed I couldn't believe what had happened and I was too scared to carry on. I later thought, 'Don't be stupid, you have to get over this and mentally train yourself.' I was OK and not hurt so I needed to get going. The better you get at motorsport and the more results you get, the more hungry you get. Accidents begin to have less effect on you as long as no-one is injured. As you roll over, you start to think that the clock is ticking on. You're racing against time and that's what keeps you going.

She also offers useful advice on relaxing in the few minutes before an event.

> My routine would start three minutes before the countdown at the stage start. I would get the helmet and gloves on and

rest my hands in my lap. I then made tight fists, as tight as I could get them and then relaxed. Every time I relaxed I could feel the tension leaving my body. By the time of the countdown I was ready for the stage.

Iain McPherson:

I make sure I eat about 1½ hours before practice or race in order to let food digest. I try to have a balance between water and energy drinks, as drinking too much water can have an adverse affect by flushing out some of the minerals in your body, which in turn have to be replaced by supplements.

After the race

This is without doubt a very important time for competitors. Even though it may be difficult, try to stick with a few basic physical and mental rules.

Make sure that you are well rehydrated. This is absolutely crucial, especially if you plan to drink any alcohol. Drink plenty of fluids but avoid sweetened drinks in the first instance, as they tend to initially dehydrate you and over stimulate your thirst centre. If you have been endurance racing and have lost a significant amount of sweat, consider adding a small amount of salt (¼ teaspoon to every litre of fluid) to replenish any sodium salts that you will have lost.

Try to avoid alcohol if you are injured during the race. The short-term treatment of acute injuries is to reduce the inflammatory process that follows by applying rest, ice, compression and elevation to the affected area. Alcohol acts in the opposite manner and makes injuries worse.

Make sure that you replenish the glycogen in the used muscles soon after the race. A rapid way of doing this is to drink a carbohydrate-rich drink that would also provide the water if dehydrated. Try also to eat a carbohydrate-rich meal if you can. The ingestion of food also serves to absorb any alcohol that you drink after the race. Suitable foods include pasta, baked potatoes, rice and noodles.

Bear in mind that competitors may be tested for drugs and alcohol up to 30 minutes after a race, and that the prescribed limit is zero.

Fitness in action – Toni Gardemeister (back) and co-driver Paavo Lukander push their car 500 metres into the time control on the 2001 New Zealand rally. (Martin Holmes Rallying)

12 **Emergency** care in motorsport

It is surprising how little competitors know of what to do in the event of an emergency and about what rescue procedures will be put into operation should they become an accident victim.

This chapter provides the reader with the fundamentals of basic life support (BLS) that should be observed whilst waiting for the medical crew to arrive, and it explains what may happen to a competitor during a rescue attempt. Vital time may be lost through an accident victim's ignorance of rescue procedures and the equipment used. Already in shock, they may be so frightened by what is happening to them that the rescue team's efforts are hindered.

Formal training in BLS, or First Aid, is recommended and in Britain courses are available through such organisations as the Red Cross and the St John Ambulance Association.

The aim of BLS is to support the casualty's Airway, Breathing and Circulation (conveniently labelled A, B and C in that order of priority) using no aids. BLS aims to preserve blood flow to the brain while waiting for definitive medical care.

Unless you are privileged to be driving Formula 1 or Indy car circuits it may take rescue and medical crews a few minutes to reach the scene of the accident. In British rallying, for example, the requirement is for

On long-stage rallies, it may take some time for the medical professionals to arrive. (Roger Bell)

rescue and medical services to be placed at the start of a special stage, or at a suitable mid-point if it is more than nine miles long. In some long-stage World Championship events, such as the Safari Rally, where stage distances of up to 140km (90 miles) are not uncommon, bad crashes can occur in remote places and it can be some time before an accident is discovered. In such cases the survival of the injured depends on those who first come upon the scene and on their ability to apply BLS.

Accident assessment

Carefully inspect the accident scene and make sure that it is safe to approach. Do not needlessly expose yourself to dangers and remember many are not immediately obvious. In circuit racing this may be other race traffic that not uncommonly head into a crashed car still on the track. In rallies there may be another vehicle seconds behind. There may be spilled fuel and the car may still be running. Every attempt should be made to turn off the engine and the electrical isolator switch on the outside of the vehicle before approaching the casualty. There may be a fire that needs to be put out before any rescue attempt can be made. Also make sure that you are wearing sufficient clothing to protect you from fuel or blood spills.

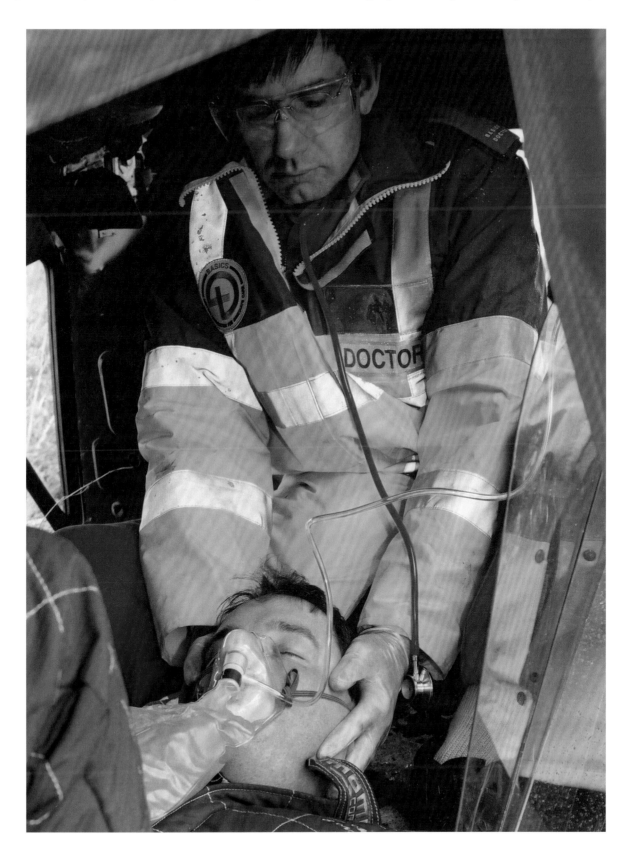

Once you consider the scene safe to approach, you can inspect the casualty. The first action is to ask if they are OK. If the answer is sensible and in a normal voice then you can assume that the:

- Airway is open and clear
- Breathing is sufficient to reply
- Circulation of blood to the brain is enough for a sensible answer to be given.

Remember that these assumptions only indicate the casualty's present condition. There can be a sudden deterioration at any time during the rescue attempt, so make sure you reassess them regularly until help arrives. In the meantime leave them in the position you find them provided they are not in further danger.

If the casualty is unconscious or if there are gurgling, wheezing, snoring or abnormal noises coming from their airway, the airway must be opened and cleared as explained below.

If you are a marshal or a competitor in an area where there are other officials about, you can ask one of them to summon rescue services once you have made the above brief assessment. This should be done through a nearby radio operator if at all possible. Accurate concise information about the type of accident, number of casualties involved, who is injured (whether competitors and/or spectators), and precise details on location should be provided if possible.

If the location is more remote and you are alone, you should provide BLS for as long as possible and flag down a passing competitor's car and get them to pass on the above information. They should stop anyway if they see an SOS board (see later). Do not worry about affecting their race time as account will be taken of this later if they have stopped for this reason. If you know that there will be no further race cars following then perform the life saving manoeuvres for about a minute before going for help.

At a motorsport event mobile phones should only be used as a last resort as confusion can arise if messages come through the 999 system rather than the established safety channels.

(A) Airway

This takes priority when dealing with anyone who is injured. If the casualty is unconscious the airway will probably be compromised as the tongue falls back and obstructs the opening to the windpipe. In an upright crashed car the unconscious competitor may be slumped forward shutting off the airway. Check and remove any obvious obstructions from their mouth, such as chewing gum, loose dentures, vomit or broken teeth. CAREFULLY lifting the jaw forwards (also known as jaw thrust) usually opens the airway by elevating the tongue off the back of the airway. It is important that you do this carefully as excessive force can cause damage to the spinal cord in the neck, especially if there is a neck fracture. AVOID LIFTING THE CHIN OR TILTING THE HEAD. Once the jaw is lifted look for signs and listen for sounds of improved breathing as the airway is opened.

Although these manoeuvres are standard practice when resuscitating other casualties, they have severe limitations in the case of an injured unconscious competitor. The limitations are discussed in the following section.

If the casualty is wearing a full-face helmet, open the visor to improve air flow. If the chin strap is digging deeply into the neck it may be shutting off the airway. Carefully loosen the strap but avoid taking the helmet off.

What about suspected neck injuries?

In motorsport accidents an unconscious driver, or in the case of high-speed impact with substantial vehicle damage especially to front and rear end, MUST be assumed to have a spinal injury to the neck. This injury can be fatal. The great Ferrari driver Gilles Villeneuve, father of Jacques Villeneuve, died of such an injury after a

  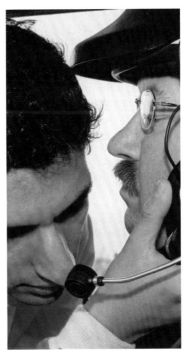 

crash during practice at Zolder in Belgium in 1982.

While trained race rescuers know what actions to perform with a suspected neck injury, it is important that bystanders or fellow competitors do not inadvertently cause any further damage. Here's a checklist of what to do, and what not to do, before the medical and rescue crew arrive:

- If at all possible try to approach the casualty from the front. This means the casualty does not have to move their head to reply to you. Any head movement is risking further spinal damage.
- Avoid chin lift or head tilt when opening the airway. These moves can damage the spinal cord if there is an unstable neck fracture already present. CAREFULLY use jaw thrust as the primary manoeuvre. LIMITED head tilt must only be used in life-threatening situations, such as when the airway is obstructed by the tongue, and things

cannot be improved by simple jaw thrust.
- Avoid moving the casualty excessively unless the situation warrants immediate removal – from a burning car, for example.
- Do not try to remove the helmet, especially if there is substantial damage to it or if there is blood seeping from the head area. Helmet removal requires trained personnel, usually including a doctor or paramedic.
- Always speak to the casualty explaining what you are doing even if they are unconscious. It calms and reassures them.

If the car is on fire and the flames are beginning to get out of control, you will have to balance the risks. Under such circumstances any reasonable action to immediately move the casualty out of danger is considered appropriate. When doing this, try to keep the casualty's head supported at all times. Avoid tilting it backwards if at all possible.

Initial assessment of someone injured. (1) Approach from the front if possible. (2) Lift jaw if casualty is unconscious or if airway sounds compromised. (3) Check for breathing by looking, listening and feeling in one simple manoeuvre. (4) Administer rescue breathing. (Roger Bell)

(B) Breathing

Once the airway is cleared, maintain the position without excessive movement of the head until help arrives. Also check that the casualty is breathing normally, i.e. there is more than just the occasional gasp.

To check for breathing follow this routine for at least 10 seconds:

- LOOK for the chest moving.
- LISTEN close to the casualty's mouth for breath sounds, and
- FEEL for breath on your cheek.

All three actions can be performed in one simple manoeuvre.

If the casualty is breathing spontaneously, maintain the airway until help arrives and move on to checking circulation. Keep checking regularly that the breathing does not deteriorate.

If the casualty is not breathing, then you must breathe for them. Make sure first that someone has already called for help. Check once again and remove any obvious obstructions from the casualty's mouth. To start ventilation deliver two effective breaths using mouth-to-mouth ventilation.

This ventilation gives the casualty around 16% oxygen from your expired breath compared to 21% that is available from normal atmospheric air. It is also known as 'rescue breathing'.

To perform it effectively the following method is suggested:

- Keep the casualty's airway open by using jaw thrust but avoiding chin lift and head tilt.
- Pinch the soft part of the nose with the index finger and thumb of one hand. This would be your right hand if rescuing a casualty from the left-hand seat of a crashed vehicle.
- Open the casualty's mouth slightly, maintaining jaw thrust.
- Having taken a deep breath seal your lips around the casualty's mouth.
- Exhale steadily for about two seconds and observe for the chest rising. Although difficult to judge, you are aiming to deliver around ¼ to 1 litre of breath.
- Allow the casualty to empty their lungs, maintaining the airway at all times. This should take about three seconds.
- Take a deep breath before each ventilation to ensure you deliver the best possible oxygen concentration.

Important notes

- If there is much resistance, then assume that the airway must still be compromised. Check in the mouth for any vomit, blood or obvious obstructions. If any are present take care in removing them, as the situation can be worsened by inadvertently forcing them further down the airway. Make sure you have an effective seal when breathing into the casualty's mouth. There should be little resistance when performing effective mouth-to-mouth ventilation.
- Ventilating too rapidly may cause air to inflate the stomach rather than the lungs.

Locating the carotid pulse in a casualty. Recent guidelines now recommend that only professional rescuers should use this to assess circulation. Lay persons and non-professional rescuers must look for signs of circulation as described on the following page.
(Roger Bell)

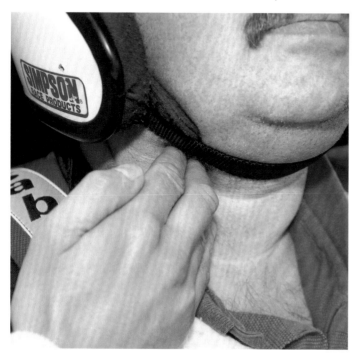

- Using large volumes of breath may also cause the stomach to inflate.
- If there is blood or vomit in the mouth, severe jaw injury, or if the rescuer's hand is not free to keep the nose pinched shut, it is acceptable to perform mouth-to-nose ventilation. In this case, seal your mouth around the casualty's nose and follow the steps outlined above. Remember to open the mouth when the casualty exhales. Mouth-to-nose ventilation may not be possible with severe nose injuries or with extensive damage to cheekbones.
- Make at least five attempts to provide two effective breaths. Do not waste too much time on any more. Move on to the assessment of the circulation.

(C) Circulation

In the past, resuscitation guidelines for lay people recommended that circulation should be assessed by feeling for a major pulse, such as the carotid pulse in the neck or femoral pulse in the groin for at least 10 seconds. While this remains true for *professional* rescuers, recent guidelines from leading organisations such as the European Resuscitation Council now recommend that lay and non-professional rescuers should simply '*look for signs of circulation*'. This recommendation followed studies that showed that even experienced rescuers can make mistakes when feeling for a major pulse.

It is now agreed that for the non-professional or lay person, an assessment of circulation should include:

- Giving two effective rescue breaths.
- Looking, listening and feeling for normal breathing, coughing or movement for no longer than 10 seconds.

If you are sure that the casualty has good signs of circulation then continue ventilating until they start breathing normally. Remember that the casualty can deteriorate at any time, so check regularly.

If there are no signs of circulation, or you are unsure then the casualty's heart has

Chest compressions. (1) Locating the xiphisternal notch in front of the chest where the ribs meet. (2) Placing the heel of the other hand two finger-breadths above the xiphisternal notch. (3) Interlocking the fingers of both hands to provide an effective method of chest compression. (4) Effective positioning over the casualty with arms straight and shoulders over the breastbone. (Roger Bell)

stopped working effectively and you must start chest compressions to get the blood circulating. For this you will need the help of someone else to hold the airway open and/or even perform rescue breathing. It may be impossible to perform the breathing and compressions in the confines of a racing cockpit or if you are alone. In this case it may be reasonable to extricate the casualty, with due attention to the neck, and undertake life support with the casualty on their back.

Chest compressions

- Locate where the ribs meet in the front of the chest and at the bottom of the breastbone (sternum) using the fingers of one hand. This area is known as the xiphisternal notch.
- Place two fingers at this point and then place the heel of the other hand next to the fingers and on the lower half of the breastbone.
- Place the heel of the first hand over the other and interlock the fingers.
- Lean over the casualty so that your shoulders are directly over your hands with your arms fully straightened.
- Firmly and smoothly press straight down on the breastbone so that it depresses about 4–5cm (1½–2 inches).
- Release the pressure keeping your hand on the breastbone so your position does not change.
- Repeat the compressions aiming for a rate of about 100 per minute or just slower than two compressions a second.

Important Dos and Don'ts

Do:
- Make sure that the chest compression time is at least 50% of each cycle (see later).
- Check for signs of circulation if the casualty makes a sudden movement or takes a breath as the heart may have started to work.

Don't:
- Apply sudden jerky movements and try to avoid bending your elbows.
- Interrupt ventilation and compression unless checking for signs of a circulation. Even in that case take no more than 10 seconds.
- Assume that feeling a pulse while doing chest compressions indicates the return of normal heart function. You are probably feeling the pressure wave from the compression.

Organising the rescuers

One-person rescue
It is difficult to decide when to get help and how much life support to perform, if any, before seeking help. There is no one answer as it depends largely on the situation. Generally speaking in trauma, however, help should be summoned after adequate resuscitation has been in place for about a minute.

A single rescuer must aim to provide 15 chest compressions after giving the initial two expired air ventilation breaths. This cycle must then be repeated.

Two-person rescue
This is more effective than single-rescue BLS as the chest compressions are not interrupted for as long. Two-person rescue may follow on from single-person rescue as someone returns from getting help.

Two-person rescue must also aim to provide 15 chest compressions for every two breaths provided. This is the latest recommendation from the European Resuscitation Council that takes over from the previous 5:1 ratio. The chest compressions must pause for only as long as it takes to provide two breaths.

What about burns?
Any competitor's biggest nightmare must be being trapped and unconscious in their rally or race car when it catches fire. This happened to Niki Lauda who suffered extensive facial burns in his accident in the

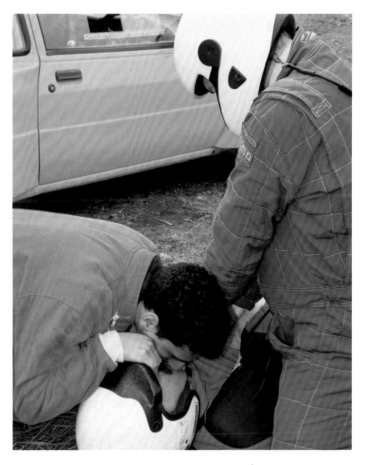

1976 German Grand Prix at Nürburgring. Amazingly, though, he escaped and went on to win the World Driver's title in 1977 and again in 1984.

FIA regulations for fire safety are justifiably very strict for all types of events and every competitor should get the best fire safety equipment affordable.

The approach to the accident vehicle on fire depends on the vehicle and event involved. In circuit and race meetings such as karting, saloon car racing and even Formula racing there are strategically placed fire safety officials and marshals as the first line of attack. In stage rallying, however, the responsibility lies with the competitors or even the spectators. Most regulations insist on having a master circuit breaker placed within arm's reach of the competitors and also located externally. These breakers, which are usually cable operated, isolate all electrical circuits of the race car, with exception of those required to operate the fire extinguishers, thereby minimising the risk of fire. The external breaker is usually mounted on the lower part of the windscreen on the driver's side. Occasionally it may be found by the rear window. In open cars it is located on the driver's side at the lower end of the main roll over bar or at the bottom of the windscreen. The breaker is marked by a red spark on a white-edged blue triangle. The 'ON' and 'OFF' positions should be clearly marked.

All racing vehicles carry a fire extinguisher or extinguishing system capable of being activated by the competitor in an emergency. The minimum requirements again depend upon the vehicle and event type. Generally, extinguishers may be hand-held or plumbed-in. They may also be manually or electrically activated. No vehicle should pass scrutineering before the race unless it meets the minimum requirements laid down by the ASN.

As with the circuit breaker, the fire system may be triggered externally by marshals, spectators or competitors

Two-person BLS.
(Roger Bell)

The results of the fiery accident in the 1976 German Grand Prix that left Niki Lauda scarred.

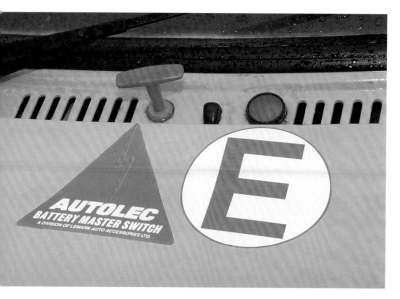

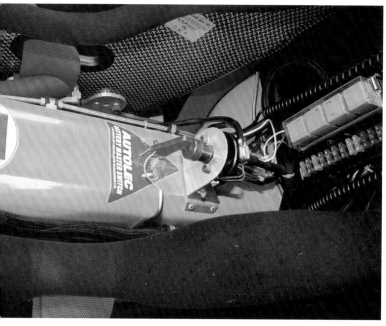

Externally and internally mounted circuit-breaker and fire-trigger on a rally car. (Roger Bell)

likely also to suffer more breathing complications than others, not only because of inhaled smoke but also because of heat injury to their airways.

Beware of those with facial burns or soot around their nostrils or in their spit. These indicate that the airway has been burned, and later swelling may result in severe breathing problems. Such casualties need to be seen by rescue and medical personnel, even though they may think they are OK at that early stage. The casualties with a wheeze or hoarse voice or difficulty swallowing may also be suffering respiratory problems.

Important Dos and Don'ts

Do:

- Remove clothing likely to continue the burning process, such as smouldering or those saturated with hot liquids.
- Remove clothing saturated with fuel or battery acid as chemical burns can be very painful.
- Remember that burnt areas swell rather quickly, so cut away or remove clothing likely to constrict.
- Make sure the casualty is kept warm especially if large amounts of water have been used to treat the burns.

Don't:

- Remove clothes stuck to burnt skin.
- Burst any blisters that may form.
- Apply excessive amounts of cold soaks or ice packs as the casualty may become hypothermic.

What competitors should expect

Overall, motorsport accidents today are relatively uncommon considering the speed and popularity of the sport, and this is mainly because of the safety measures now mandatory with most forms of the sport. When accidents do occur, any emergency is normally handled promptly and effectively by well-trained rescue and medical crews.

themselves. The trigger should be located next to, or in some cases combined with, the circuit breaker. It is marked by the letter 'E' in red on a white circle.

Dealing with burns

As with other forms of rescue, do not attempt to rescue a casualty until a fire or the risk of a fire has been dealt with effectively. Remember that although the fire itself may have been doused, the casualty may still be burning because of smouldering clothes. Burns casualties are

However, it is important that drivers are aware of standard emergency procedures. When trapped and in pain, most people will exhibit a 'fight or flight' response, especially if they are in shock or drifting in and out of consciousness. But if they are familiar with rescue crew routine, even if the communicating language is not in their mother tongue, they are more likely to co-operate than hinder progress by struggling. They will learn to expect certain questions from the rescue and medical staff, and they will effectively take part in their own rescue.

If trapped and conscious

Motorsport accidents occur so quickly that there is little that can be done until the car comes to a stop. Only then can an account be taken of what has happened.

A driver's initial thoughts (invariably following a few choice words) are usually those of disbelief. Then their own safety becomes a priority as they take stock of what state they (and their co-driver if present) are in. Pain will probably not be felt immediately because of the levels of adrenaline and other hormones in their system. Most then try to scramble free from their car fearing fire or being crashed into by following cars, and if they find they are trapped there is a tendency to panic, and most will struggle to free themselves from whatever is trapping them. It is at this point that the pain of any injury will be felt.

How the driver is trapped will depend on the type of crash. With head-on accidents the footwell may buckle onto the feet, or the steering wheel and column may move towards the torso. In saloon car rollovers, the roof may have buckled severely limiting movement within the cockpit.

When will help arrive?

The response times and the make up of the emergency units present at the event will

The notorious Corsica Rally claims yet another casualty. Colin McRae's and Nicky Grist's infamous crash that led to some questions being asked about provision of rescue services at certain rally events. (Maurice Selden, Martin Holmes Rallying)

The Race Rescue Unit on standby at a Formula 1 race meeting. (Mike Gibbon, MVG Photographic)

At multi-use stage rallies there will be a similar Rally Rescue Unit as well as a Recovery Unit at each stage start. Stages longer than nine miles will have a similar set-up at a suitable mid-point. These all are minimum requirements and in many cases higher standards will be achieved.

The Rescue Unit

This vehicle is a fully equipped ambulance able to carry at least one fully immobilised casualty, and probably one other 'walking wounded'. It has all of the equipment a standard county ambulance would have, with additional advanced life support equipment for use by the associated paramedic or doctor. It also carries tools for facilitating safe extrication described later in this section. The personnel are experienced in rally marshalling, advanced first-aid and in the handling of all the cutting equipment.

The Recovery Unit

Traditionally, this vehicle tidied up at the end of a rally stage, recovering wrecks after the stage was over, and towing them out. Like many of the safety disciplines in modern motorsport, the crews have become much more professional and now have an important role in the primary response, providing additional vehicle stabilisation and dismantling skills. Also, extra pairs of experienced hands are always useful at an incident.

While accidents are rapidly detected at speed and circuit events, during multi-use stage rallies it may take several minutes before the rescue and medical teams are notified and mobilised. If not already reported over the radio or mobile phone by the competitors themselves, the following race cars will usually report the accident to race officials at the stage finish. In the UK all competitors are required to carry an A4 size white board with a red coloured SOS on one side and a green OK on the other. The SOS should be displayed to following competitors if medical assistance is required and the OK if the crew is safe.

depend upon the event type and the regulations laid down by the ASN.

As an example, in Britain at a race or speed event, Race Rescue units with a doctor or MSA-registered paramedic aim to be at the scene of the accident within about 90 seconds of leaving their standby position.

It may happen to you

If you are unfortunate enough to crash, and find yourself trapped, it is important that you try to keep calm. Take stock of what injuries, if any, you have sustained and think of how you can aid your own rescue.

Try to apply to yourself, if possible, the same principles of Airway, Breathing and Circulation mentioned earlier in this section. How is your breathing (or that of your co-driver)? Take a deep and gentle breath in. Is that painful? If so it could indicate damage to your ribs and chest wall. Try to avoid taking your helmet off and moving your head excessively in case you have an undiagnosed neck fracture. Keep your head in a neutral position and especially avoid tilting your head back. A neck fracture may sound impossible but I have dealt with a fully conscious casualty after a road traffic accident who was discovered to have an unstable neck fracture several hours after his transfer to hospital. In fact he had already been through the local hospital before being transferred by helicopter to our surgical team. In the meantime no attention was paid to his neck. He was very fortunate to have no resulting damage.

Do you have any tingling sensations or weakness in your limbs? Any localised pain will probably give you a fair idea of what you have injured. Very gently try to move your legs and feet as they are the most likely to be trapped. If you have any severe pain or can feel abnormal grating sensations then stop as this could indicate fractures. Try also not to twist your spine too much as you wait for help, especially if doing so causes numbness and tingling in your limbs. Qualified rescue crews are trained to suspect a spinal injury in all such accidents and will extricate you from the vehicle using special equipment designed to keep your spine protected at all times.

Also try to take stock of how safe the vehicle is for those trying to rescue you. An early priority of a rescue crew chief who controls a rescue attempt is to ensure stability of the vehicle. You can aid this process by telling him whether the car is precariously balanced or safe to approach. Also let him know if there has been a fuel spill or if you managed to isolate the race car electrics after the accident.

It is important that the attending medical staff also know whether you have suffered any burns or if you were exposed to any smoke. Burns and suspected smoke inhalation injuries require special care and management that is best started early.

There will be questions that the doctor or paramedic may also ask you. These will be about whether you have any allergies, your tetanus status, the last time you had anything to eat or drink and any significant medical history they should be aware of.

Almost certainly the first question you will be asked will be '*Are you OK?*' As a member of a race rescue crew it is reassuring to be told, '*I'm OK! I don't think I was knocked out. I'm sore when I breathe in deeply on the right side of my chest though. I can't move my right leg – I think it is trapped!*' or something along

The red SOS card displayed prominently on the car for the attention of passing vehicles. The OK sign is green. (Roger Bell)

those lines. Not only does that indicate that the casualty has a patent airway, adequate breathing and reasonable blood circulation to the brain, they have taken account of what has happened to them and what needs attention. On the other hand an aggressive and unco-operative casualty may be an indication of advanced blood loss that necessitates immediate removal and attention, probably not in the smooth and painless manner that would have otherwise been the case.

Who will get to you first?

This depends largely on the event type and regulations local to you. In the UK, for example, the emergency unit may consist of the Medical and Race Rescue Unit in the same vehicle. Many rally and hill climb events have this set up. In some circuit events, such as Formula 1 races, there may be a Fast Doctor Car that acts as a first response unit and provides immediate casualty care while the Rescue Unit is on its way. Recently First Intervention Vehicles (FIVs) have been introduced to international rallying. Like Fast Doctor Cars they provide basic casualty care until the Race Rescue Unit arrives. Occasionally a Snatch Vehicle may be employed to move the stranded accident vehicle from danger

Some of the powered tools likely to be encountered during a rescue attempt – electric saw; pneumatic air chisel; combination cutters and spreaders and a helmet saw.
(Roger Bell)

before any attention can be paid to the casualty.

The Race Rescue Unit

The Race Rescue Unit normally consists of a crew chief, two tool operators and a spare man who may also double up as an assistant to the doctor. Their services are normally voluntary. The unit is led by the crew chief, whose role is essentially to control and co-ordinate the rescue attempt. He will be the one directing the rescue crew and delegating tasks. If there is no doctor present he will allocate a member of the team to fulfil that role while he makes an initial assessment of the scene, its safety and vehicle damage. He will then report to the doctor the condition of the casualty, nature of entrapment and preferred method and speed of extrication.

If the entrapment is complex, the crew chief's priority is to create enough space for the medical crew to work in and stabilise the casualty. Once the extrication plan is decided on, the chief then stabilises the vehicle, if required, by means of ropes, props or belts. Generally, assuming the crew is sufficient and competent, the chief will have to do little 'hands-on' work, lending only the occasional hand. His role is essentially supportive and supervisory.

The equipment

The aim of using equipment is to create enough space in a safe manner so that the trapped and injured casualty can be removed without further harm and damage.

Race Rescue Units carry a tremendous amount of equipment designed to extricate even the most awkwardly trapped casualty. The equipment can be broadly classified as either powered or hand tools. Once the extrication plan is decided, one member of the team will be assigned to assemble the heavier power tools while the others will probably begin work using hand tools such as hacksaws and Stanley knives. Before any work is started, however, the medically stabilised casualty will be protected from

flying debris either by plastic transparent shields or blankets.

Electric generators, bottled air or hydraulics may power the tools. In either case they are extremely noisy, especially when working in a confined space as they are likely to be. The types of powered tools found in Race Rescue Units commonly include air or electric saws, helmet saws, air chisels (Zip guns), spreaders and cutters.

The saws are versatile and can be used for cutting through pillars of the accident vehicle. They generate a fair amount of vibration and noise, and if close to the casualty may cause nausea and vomiting. Air chisels are normally used for cutting through door panels, while combination cutters and spreaders, either hand or power operated, are useful for bursting open hinges or cutting through most materials. They are extremely powerful tools that are treated with utmost respect by the rescue crew. Although the jaws move slowly, they exert extremely high pressures that can be difficult to control. It is therefore essential that you keep well clear of their working ends.

Other hydraulic tools include pedal cutters, designed to free trapped feet from distorted foot wells and cut through steering wheels, and rams that can lift collapsed engine bulkheads that commonly result from front-end impacts. The pedal cutter will be used in close proximity to the trapped casualty and it is essential that the casualty co-operate fully to prevent injury. While the hydraulic tools are being operated you will hear various commands such as '*pump*' and '*release*' being shouted to the pump operator by the rescuer positioning the working ends of the tool.

In some cases it will be necessary to cut the helmet from a conscious casualty using a helmet saw. The cutting blade of a helmet saw is usually circular. It oscillates at a high frequency and only cuts when applied to a solid object. It will therefore not cut into human skin or tissue unless the blade is pressed on skin over a bone, e.g. the jaw. If such a tool is being used on you please try to co-operate fully with the rescuer. Application of the saw blade to the helmet is very noisy and results in vibrations that may disorientate you.

Basic extrication strategies

The strategies discussed below are largely relevant to motorsport vehicles that resemble conventional road going vehicles. The principles of extrication are, however, the same for all other forms of racing vehicles.

To gain access to the casualty and ensure their safe removal, the accident vehicle can

The combination hydraulically-operated cutter and spreader seen cutting through a door pillar and roll cage of a competition car with apparent ease. (Roger Bell)

Hydraulically operated pedal cutters for cutting through a steering wheel. (Roger Bell)

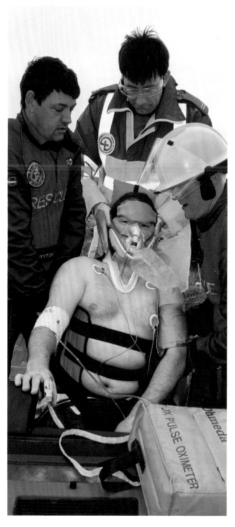

A de-roofed competition car with the casualty being lifted vertically using a spinal protection device. (Roger Bell)

Folding down the side of a racing car on its roof. This is a useful method of gaining access to the casualty from the side. (Roger Bell)

be entered either through the roof or from the side. The vehicle may be completely de-roofed by first removing the front and rear windscreens, if present. Rescue crews are trained to avoid breaking glass and will try to remove the windscreens fully intact if possible. The car pillars are then cut as low as possible to door level. The last pillar to be cut is usually the one next to the occupant. Once the vehicle is de-roofed the casualty can be lifted easily, with due attention to the spine.

A quicker alternative to de-roofing and one that requires fewer personnel is called 'flapping the roof' – a similar process to opening a can of sardines whereby the front two pairs of pillars are cut and the roof is peeled back. Another strategy that is particularly useful when the racing car is on its side involves flapping the roof sideways and down. This technique is especially beneficial when the head of the casualty is lying against the pillar closest to him.

Another technique for gaining access is through the side of the racing car. Once the side door or doors have been opened, forcefully or otherwise, the central pillar of the car is cut close to the roof. Intersecting cuts are then made into the chassis on either side of the central pillar and the pillar bent down to lie flat or cut out altogether.

The Medical Rescue Unit

A paramedic or qualified doctor will probably make up the Medical Rescue Unit. In the UK, the doctor will probably be dressed in red overalls with the paramedic in green overalls. In some instances the medical staff will travel in a separate vehicle, but they may arrive with the Race Rescue Unit. The doctor will make an assessment of the casualty on arrival and deal immediately with any life-threatening conditions. Once the casualty is stabilised, an assessment will also be made of the degree of entrapment and how rapidly the doctor wishes the casualty to be extricated.

The doctor will follow the same priorities of Airway, Breathing and Circulation described in the earlier section. Only this time, with medical aids at hand, there will be more intervention.

Assuming you are conscious and orientated, your coherent replies to the doctor's queries will indicate that at least your airway, breathing and circulation are intact for the moment. The doctor and an assistant will attempt to take off your helmet in a controlled manner. You will be requested not to move your head while it is being supported in a neutral position by a crew member. The chin strap will be cut or undone and the helmet removed either from the rear or front, at all times keeping the head supported. DO NOT INTERFERE WITH THIS IMPORTANT MANOEUVRE EVEN THOUGH YOU THINK YOUR NECK IS OK.

A stiff collar will then be applied around your neck that will restrict your neck movements. That is exactly what it is designed to do, so do not panic. Even once this is done a crew member will continue to support your head, and it is possible that your ears may be covered by his hands as this is being done.

At this stage, if not before, an oxygen mask may be applied to your face. These masks can be claustrophobic, but forewarned is forearmed! Alternatively, the doctor may elect to deliver oxygen using tubing that is inserted only slightly into the nose. In either case you will hear the constant hiss of oxygen being delivered. Again, do not fight this essential manoeuvre that all trained paramedics and doctors must perform in a situation similar to yours. The doctor will probably feel for a major pulse, most likely in your neck, to estimate the status of your circulation. This can be uncomfortable as sometimes the pulse is difficult to locate, especially if a stiff collar is in place and you are sitting upright. There may be some prodding in your neck for a few seconds, and once the pulse is located it may be felt for up to 10 seconds. Of course, the doctor will be explaining exactly what is happening at every stage, but from personal experience, with hands over your ears and the hissing of oxygen it is sometimes difficult to comprehend much of what is being said.

The doctor or paramedic will try to insert an intravenous line into your arm. Again, this practice is essential, as fluids have to be provided rapidly to someone in your circumstances. The location of choice

Removal of the helmet from the front while the head is being supported by a crew member. This is easier with an open-face helmet, but a closed helmet may require the use of a helmet cutter, and application of a stiff collar designed to limit damage to the spinal cord if a neck fracture is present. Note that an oxygen mask has been placed on the face and the head is still held in a neutral position.
(Roger Bell)

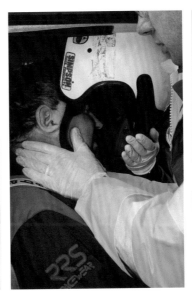

Insertion of an intravenous line into a vein in the arm. A tourniquet, which is removed once the line is in place, can be seen on the upper arm. The second photo shows the arm being splinted and the line secured.
(Roger Bell)

is on the inside of your elbow. Insertion may first involve cutting your race suit arm to gain access. A tourniquet will then be applied to your upper arm to 'raise a vein' and the line inserted with a sharp needle. Most people feel only a jab when the line is inserted. The line will then be taped down and a flat board strapped to your arm in some circumstances. This board prevents you from bending your elbow and kinking the line as fluids run into you.

There are possible life-threatening

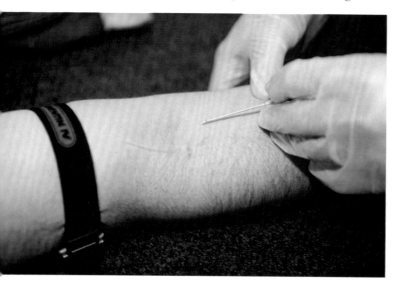

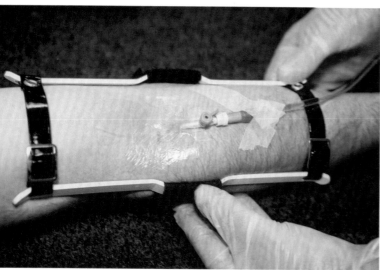

emergencies that trained medical staff must check for and exclude before considering you sufficiently stable for extrication. This involves examining your chest, best done by cutting off your race suit and underwear with heavy-duty scissors. While the doctor listens to your heart and lungs using a stethoscope, try not to speak to him. Instead, take in normal breaths with your mouth open. Part of the chest examination will involve carefully feeling your chest wall. Do let the doctor know what part is tender, if any, as this will help him focus on that particular area.

At some point a light will be shone into your eyes to check the size of your pupils. This gives the doctor an idea of whether any severe internal head damage is present. To make sure your spine has not been damaged, you will probably be asked if you have any weaknesses or 'pins and needles' feeling in your arms or legs. You may also be asked to wriggle your toes or fingers to make sure the nerves are intact.

Some medical equipment may well be attached to monitor you as you are being extricated or transferred. A blood pressure cuff to your upper arm and an oxygen saturation monitor on your finger are commonly used. Also, if the doctor feels it appropriate, he may attach three heart leads to your chest wall to record your heart's electric activity. This may be necessary if you have suffered a heavy front-end impact, or complain of pain in the front of your chest wall, or if it is suspected that you have fractured your breastbone.

Pain relief

Strong painkillers, such as morphine, may also be given through the intravenous line but only by an attending doctor. Usually within several seconds of receiving of a morphine-based drug, some people encounter a tingling sensation lasting seconds over most of their body. Some also experience nausea and vomiting. The drug itself is a potent painkiller that works within minutes if administered through an intravenous line. It may, however, make you feel drowsy.

Another relatively potent painkiller is Entonox, a 50:50 mixture of oxygen and nitrous oxide (also known as 'laughing gas'). It is delivered through a special demand valve that requires a good seal around the mouth and fairly deep breathing to open the valve. If the doctor suspects a skull fracture or a pneumothorax (air in the chest but outside the lung), then Entonox is not suitable. An advantage of Entonox is that it does not require a doctor to provide it.

Occasionally the doctor may choose to infiltrate local anaesthetic around a large nerve to numb the affected area. An example is a pain from a fractured thighbone, which can be dulled with a quick and often painless injection close to the femoral nerve in the groin. This injection is useful before putting the leg into a splint.

Extrication

The speed and method of removal is dictated largely by your condition and any surrounding risks. Clearly if there is a life-threatening emergency, such as a fire, that calls for immediate removal then you will be extricated with speed but in a controlled manner to prevent further injury. In this situation the decision to evacuate immediately is made by the doctor or paramedic who will probably support your neck and head during the extrication process. This is known as the *scoop and run* decision, where it is felt that, on balance, you will fare better if removed from immediate danger even though it means a risk of injury to your neck or spine.

In other situations, almost every trapped casualty will be removed with neck protection (as described earlier) and using devices designed to protect the spine. Rescue and medical teams constantly practise all forms of removal using available protection devices in various scenarios until every procedure is conducted smoothly.

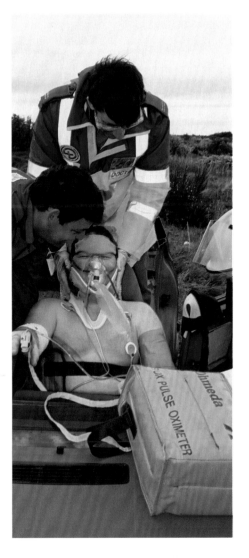

A casualty being stabilised while still trapped. Heart monitoring leads, an oxygen saturation probe and a blood-pressure cuff are seen attached to the competitor whose clothes have been cut off. It is evident that within a short time a lot of equipment, largely foreign to the casualty, will be used in a relatively confined space. (Roger Bell)

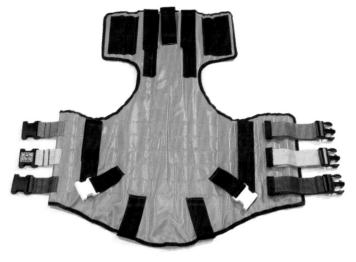

A KED, which has a supporting head cushion and straps for tightening around the chest and crutch. (Ferno)

Spinal extrication devices include names such as KED, TED and RED. They all have a similar purpose, which is to immobilise and splint your spine while moving you. The use of such devices is now mandatory for FIA events.

Applying a spinal extrication device involves teamwork and practice. Most of all, it requires co-operation from the casualty who may or may not think the procedure is necessary. As the device is being applied you will be asked to move in your seat while at all times keeping the profile of your spine unchanged. The devices also have straps that need to be fairly tight to prevent slippage when extricating. Let the teams know if the straps are too constrictive or painful as some are tightened in the crutch area.

An attempt will be made to lift you in one clean movement and without bending your back. DO NOT TRY TO HELP THE RESCUE CREW AT THIS MOMENT.

Once you have been removed from the vehicle, you will be lowered onto a long board and strapped tightly for transfer. At

A long board with the casualty strapped tightly in ready for transfer. The head has been fully immobilised using head blocks and a Velcro-based strap across the forehead.
(Roger Bell)

this point your head may be fully immobilised using head blocks and a strap across your forehead. The spinal board is exceedingly hard and uncomfortable and has been known to cause pressure sores in casualties within as little as 20 minutes.

The purpose of the long board is to facilitate transfer onto a vacuum mattress so you should not be on the board for more than a few minutes. Transfer onto the mattress is a single co-ordinated movement that assumes full co-operation from the casualty. Once placed on the vacuum mattress, air will be sucked out of the device, which then moulds itself fully around the body. The vacuum mattress is extremely effective and almost rock-hard when fully deflated. It completely immobilises you and it can be uncomfortable on long journeys. In some cases, there may be no vacuum mattress and transport will be on a spinal board. Do let the attending staff know if you are in pain from the area of your body in contact with the board.

In some circumstances it will be difficult to transfer a seriously injured casualty on a spinal board owing to uneven, rough ground or steep banks. Scoop stretchers allow casualty transport over such terrain but offer little protection for the spine as the weight of the casualty makes the stretcher flex. A rather painful complication of scoop stretchers is nipping of skin as the stretcher is applied or set down.

Where do you go?

In most speed and race events you will be transported to the ambulance which will then proceed to the local hospital. In some cases, such as rallies, the Rescue Unit may have to transfer you to a pre-determined rendezvous point where an ambulance may be waiting. In other cases helicopter evacuation to hospital may be the fastest and most appropriate, especially if one is on stand-by or has been scrambled because of the nature and severity of the injuries.

Evacuation to the hospital is no fun if

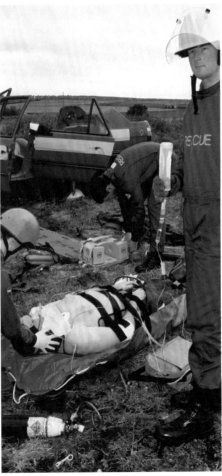

A vacuum mattress before use and with the casualty strapped in. (Roger Bell)

The two halves of a scoop stretcher being applied to a casualty for transport. The stretcher is useful for steep inclines or rough terrain as long as the casualty is strapped on, as shown in the second photo.
(Roger Bell)

you are in pain, strapped tightly to a spinal board or vacuum mattress and cannot move your head even in the slightest. To make matters worse you may have a tendency to motion sickness or are reacting to the analgesic and are feeling nauseated. Do let the staff know if you are feeling sick as they will have to undo the head straps and support your head in readiness. Being sick while lying immobilised face up is not the greatest feeling!

Helicopter evacuation poses its own problems and a high degree of safety is essential. When Didier Pironi, the Formula 1 Ferrari driver, was being transferred to the race helicopter following his massive crash in Hockenheim in 1982 that ended his racing career, an umbrella was being used to protect his body from heavy rain. As the stretcher party approached the helicopter the top of the umbrella caught the main rotor blades damaging them. The bearer was considered lucky not to have been decapitated!

During helicopter transfer noise levels and vibration are usually very high and occasionally uncomfortable. If not already applied, ask for ear defenders. It may be useful to have pre-determined signals ready for use in case you experience increasing pain and discomfort. Another potential problem is to do with flicker from the rotors. While it can occasionally lead to fits, it may more commonly cause vertigo.

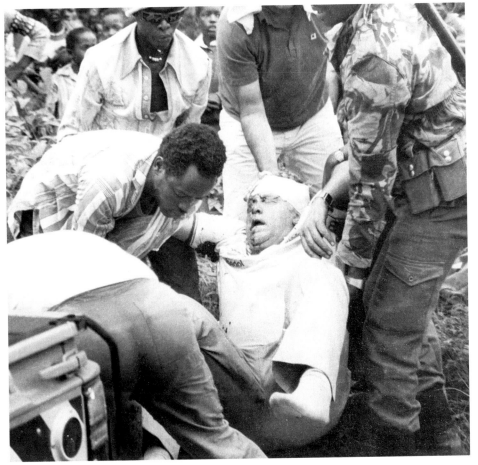

The rescue of Hans Schuller in the 1985 Safari Rally from his overturned Nissan 240 RS. Fortunately, motorsport medical rescue and extrication has come a long way since then in most events. The driver is clearly unconscious with a bleeding head wound indicating substantial trauma to the head and neck. Yet there is little or no attention being paid to his cervical spine during transfer. There are still many national events which provide less than ideal casualty care for the competitors. In some events lives could have been saved if bystanders and officials had been better educated and informed. (Anwar Sidi, Sidi's)

13 Getting a licence to compete

The FIA (Fédération Internationale de l'Automobile) based in Geneva, Switzerland, is the leading international body that makes and enforces rules relating to automobile competitions. The rules are drawn up in a document called the International Sporting Code which, along with its appendices, can be viewed on the FIA's website (www.fia.com) or in the FIA Yearbook. Each country taking part in motorsport has a club or federation known as an ASN (National Automobile Club) that can affiliate itself to the FIA. The ASN is then bound by the rules of the Code and enforces them at national level. In the British Isles (excluding the Republic of Ireland) the ASN is the MSA (Motor Sports Association) based at Colnbrook, England. Its website is www.msauk.org.

Each ASN may draw up its own regulations. The MSA's regulations can be found in the *MSA Competitors' Yearbook* (known as 'The Blue Book'). Although they may be worded differently they all comply more or less with the Code issued by the FIA. In the UK the regulations are also reviewed by the British government's Office of Fair Trading to make sure the practices are satisfactory.

Who can and cannot race?

First, check with your ASN about age eligibility, as there are certain minimum age limits that apply depending upon the type of event entered.

Also, competing in motorsport events can be precluded by some medical conditions. For FIA international status events these include instances where limb movement is restricted by more than 50%; where there have been amputations (except where fingers are lost but grip function in both hands is retained); where orthopaedic prostheses are used (the resulting function being not normal or near normal); and where epilepsy exists and is still under treatment or where there is an associated behavioural affect. Many ASNs, including the MSA, may take a more lenient approach, so it is worth checking with your local ASN if you are not sure.

Other conditions may require a medical assessment by someone approved by the ASN before a licence can be issued. These include insulin-dependent diabetes, heart valve problems and angina. Those who have had a heart attack or have suffered from other heart conditions, have orthopaedic prostheses, have limited hand movement or have existing psychiatric conditions are also assessed individually.

If you are in doubt about an existing medical condition, contact your ASN which may have a specialist advisory panel to help. Remember, ASNs do not set out to fail everyone who applies, and they will work with you to reach, it is hoped, a favourable decision.

The medical examination

It goes without saying that motorsport can be dangerous, and racing places a great strain on the system. High body-temperature, vehicle vibration, muscular and emotional stress all have to be contended with. Heart rates close to 200 beats per minute have been

Licensed to compete! A club rally car in action. (Mike Gibbon, MVG Photographic)

122

recorded even in professional drivers, and essentially they are far fitter than amateur competitors. These stresses are tolerated better if you are mentally relaxed, well hydrated and physically fit. But, for example, anyone with a hidden heart complaint would be unlikely to withstand them and might suffer irreversible damage, or even death, while competing. The medical examination is designed to detect such weaknesses so that they can be given early treatment and, it is hoped, thereby restoring the chance to race. The examination's purpose is not to fail all but the fittest, and I say this as a doctor performing routine medicals and a driver

who receives medical examinations. In my experience there is little that will fail someone outright that he or she does not already know about.

Appendix L of the International Sporting Code clearly states the need for a medical examination to obtain an international licence from the ASN, and an annual one thereafter. It is no concern of the FIA how or to whom an ASN issues licences for events at national level, as these events do not fall within FIA jurisdiction. Each ASN is entitled to apply its own rules and some are stricter than others. In Britain this regulation is met by requesting all applicants to complete an annual self-declaration of medical fitness. A medical examination and eye test is recommended if the applicant has not had either of these recently. Certain applicants, such as those applying for a Car, Truck or Kart licence, over the age of 18, must have a medical examination. This may be followed by an annual self-declaration until age 45, after which competitors must pass a medical examination each year.

Although the format of the medical examination may vary from country to country, for international licences the FIA has stipulated the minimum requirements for each examination. Each applicant must have an eyesight test and orthopaedic examination (essentially looking at their limbs and spine functions). Also, those aged 45 and over must have a stress ECG performed to ensure there are no heart problems. This test involves the use of a treadmill in accordance with a set protocol over a specified time. The results of a stress ECG are valid for two years. Some national authorities may also insist on details of blood groups for each applicant, along with urine tests.

Medical regulations change all the time to allow for individual cases. It will be worth asking your local ASN about any new rules that may affect you. For example, the MSA has amended its regulations regarding eyesight standards after consulting with specialists to allow many competitors with monocular vision to compete.

The MSA Annual Medical Form that covers the medical examination regulations laid down by the FIA. A copy of the form is printed in the Blue Book.

Disabled drivers

Disabled drivers in motor sport, although uncommon, are not entirely unheard of. The Australian Mark Pope who, sadly, was rendered paraplegic by a motocross accident when he was 16, has not only competed in the Paralympics but has driven in rallies, sometimes finishing as high as second position in his class. Another example is Britain's David Butler, a triple amputee, who has qualified for full Race and Rally licences. The FIA does issue special licences for drivers who have a congenital or acquired handicap as long as certain criteria are met. For example, applicants must have a full medical evaluation of their disabilities and they must modify their vehicles as indicated by the ASN. An evaluation must also be made of their ability to extract themselves from an automobile in an emergency situation. The rules set out by the FIA state: '… *he must move from a sitting to a standing position, turn easily over both ways; must be able to extricate himself vertically using an arm, and in the same way be able to exit laterally.*'

There are special competition rules for handicapped drivers and these depend largely on a competitor's former and current driving skills. It is best to check with the ASN whether any events are running for handicapped drivers or whether you qualify to compete alongside non-handicapped drivers. The latter will depend upon your skills and requires assessment by the FIA Medical Commission and Circuits and Safety Commission.

Special organisations have been established to represent disabled drivers wishing to compete in motorsport. One of these is the British Motorsport Association for the Disabled (BMSAD). Set up in 1987, it has helped over 100 competitors gain the right to compete in various motorsport events.

Doping

The FIA and all affiliated organisations are clear on their policy with regard to doping. International competitors found to test positive in FIA-sanctioned events are reported either directly or indirectly to the President of the FIA. Offences that are serious can be judged directly by the FIA without involvement of the local ASN. In national events, however, the ASN may deal with the matter entirely.

The MSA randomly tests for drugs and alcohol, and any competitor testing positive is reported to the MSA. If the test results are upheld they will be asked to appear before an MSA tribunal and they will be reported to the Sports Council.

The International Olympic Committee (IOC) regularly reviews the list of substances and methods open to abuse. The updates may be viewed on the FIA website. Motorsport bodies generally use the IOC list of banned substances, with the important addition of alcohol. It is worth paying the site a visit to find out what may happen if you are requested to provide a sample for analysis. Your ASN or the FIA may request samples. The President of the FIA also has the authority to request spot checks not only during competitions but also at any time. Any competitor failing to comply will be subject to sanctions.

Some general advice

Along with what the FIA states in its regulations, the following general advice is also useful.

You should know your blood group and tetanus status. If you have not been immunised against tetanus you are strongly advised to have this done. Competitors with life-threatening allergies, especially to antibiotics, should wear identity tags detailing the allergy, and it is recommended that you tell the event medical officer of your condition before competing. The same advice applies to asthmatics and those who require special medical treatment. If you are in any doubt about your pre-existing condition, then early liaison with the event doctor will guard against any problems should an emergency arise.

All motorsport bodies advise against chewing gum while racing as this could become caught in the throat and cause an airway blockage. For the same reason false dentures should be removed.

References

ABC of Sports Medicine, McLatchie, G., BMJ Publishing, London, 2000.

Almond, L. & Newberry, I. 'The importance of physical activity in weight management'. *Obesity in Practice*. 2:10-12; 2000.

Allied Dunbar National Fitness Survey – Main Findings. London: Sports Council and Health Education Authority, 1992.

Armstrong *et al*. 'Urinary Indices of Hydration Status'. *International Journal of Sports Nutrition* 1994; 4:265-79.

Bertrand, C., Keromes, A., Lemeunier, B. F., Meistelmann, C., Prieur, C. & Richalet, J. P. Physiologie des Sports Mécanques, *1st International Congress of Sport Automobile, Marseilles*, 1983 in *Life at the Limit*, Sid Watkins, Macmillan Publishers, London, 1996.

Brukner, P. & Khan, K. *Clinical Sports Medicine*, McGraw-Hill Company, Australia, 2000.

Cooper, K. H., 'A means of assessing maximum oxygen uptake'. *Journal of the American Medical Association*, 1968; 203:201-204.

Health Education Authority. *Managing Weight*. A workbook for health and other professionals. London: Health Education Authority, 1998.

In Pursuit of Excellence. How to win in sport and life through mental training. Orlick, T., Human Kinetics, Champaign, 2000.

Kline, G., Pocari, J., Hintermeister, R., Freedson, P., Ward, A., McCarron, R., Ross, J. & Rippe, J. 'Estimation of VO_2 max from a one-mile track walk, gender, age, and body weight'. *Medicine and Science in Sports and Exercise, 1987*; 19:253-259.

Lakka, T., Venalainen, J., Rauramaa, R., Salonen, R., Tuomilehto, J. & Salonen, J. 'Relation of leisure-time physical activity and cardiorespiratory fitness to the risk of acute myocardial infarction in men'. *New England Journal of Medicine*, 1994; 330:1549-1554.

Life at the Limit, Sid Watkins, Macmillan Publishers, London, 1996.

Rasch, W. & Cabanac, M. 'Selective brain cooling is affected by wearing headgear during exercise'. *Journal of Applied Physiology* 1993; 74:1229.

Rolls, B. T. *et al*. 'Thirst following water deprivation in humans'. *American Journal of Physiology* 1980; 239:476.

Sharkey, B. J. *Fitness and Health, 4th edition*, Human Kinetics, Champaign, 1997.

The Complete Guide to Sports Nutrition, Anita Bean, (3rd edition), A. & C. Black, London, 2000.

World Health Organisation. 'Obesity – promoting and managing the global epidemic'. *Report of a WHO consultation on obesity*. Geneva WHO 1998.

Index